# Bards Annual 2019

## The Annual Publication of the Bards Initiative

## Bards Initiative

James P. Wagner (Ishwa)—Editor, Compiler

Nick Hale—Submissions Editor, Compiler

Marc Rosen—Associate Editor

J R Turek—Associate Editor

Cover Art: Vincent (VinVulpis) Brancato

Layout Design: James P. Wagner (Ishwa)

Bards Annual 2019

Copyright © 2019 by The Bards Initiative

Published by Local Gems Press

www.localgemspoetrypress.com

*Editing and technical assistance:*

*Judy Turek*

*msjevus@optonline.net*

# Foreword

Welcome again, Long Island poets to Bards Annual! 2019 marks the 9th year of Bards Annual, and 9 years of the Bards Initiative on Long Island. There have been so many amazing things during this golden age of Long Island poetry.

Bards Against Hunger, now a national entity, continues to grow. The tradition that we started here on LI of poets gathering food for local food banks has caught on as far away as California and Manchester England.

NoVA Bards, our long-time sister group is coming up on its fifth year anniversary. Many of you have enjoyed their poetry at our annual Bards/NoVA Bards reading where we read poems from both anthologies. We've also seen the rise of chapters in other states this year, with small anthologies happening in New Jersey, Pennsylvania and Connecticut.

And not to mention the celebration of Walt Whitman's Bicentennial, the 3 day convention right here on Long Island that brought poets and poetry fans from as far away as Los Angeles. We launched 2 books to celebrate Whitman's Legacy, and over the course of the weekend, over 400 people were in attendance.

Long Island poets even got to meet a congregation from our sister-chapter NoVA Bards who made the journey north for the special event.

It seems like every day new people join our community. And each one adds their own unique voice to the ever growing treasure-trove of the Long Island Poetry Community. Enjoy the 9th edition of Bards Annual!

~ James P. Wagner (Ishwa)
President, Bards Initiative.

# Table of Contents

# Introduction

Welcome to the ninth year of Bards Annual.

This also year marks the fifth anniversary of NoVA Bards, where I live in Northern Virginia. During these past five years, using the example of the Long Island poetry community, our little group has grown into a large and thriving community of poets. We've also reached out an interacted, in dozens of little ways, with the Long Island poetry community. Most notably, each year, the Bards Initiative holds a special reading where Long Island poets read from both NoVA Bards and Bards Annual, a tradition which we have finally started in NoVA as well.

This is what made travelling to the Walt Whitman Bicentennial with a group of NoVA poets so exciting. Our reading, which took place early on Saturday morning, was one of the most well attended non-anthology reading of the convention. One poet mentioned being approached by people she'd never interacted with before and greeted with "It's so nice to finally meet you!"

The Bicentennial was both the culmination of five years of sharing and collaboration as well as the start of an exciting, more connected and collaborative future. Between the growth NoVA Bards has seen, our collaborations with other existing poetry groups, and the new friends we've made through the various other regional bards anthologies published this year, there's a lot to look forward to. However, as exciting as the future is, there's plenty to celebrate in the present.

~ Nick Hale
Vice President, Bards Initiative

# Lloyd Abrams

## on the charm city circulator

to visit the art museum of baltimore
and the edgar allan poe house and his gravesite
we get on the charm city circulator
at the corner opposite a whole foods market

on this sweltering august day
in our blue and chartreuse white-roofed coach
we're joined by some other tourists
taking advantage of the cost-free ride
along with several junkies nodding off
a trio of young girls holding babies not much younger
a cluster of teenagers shuckin' and jivin'
and a gaggle of street people yakkin' it up
using the air-conditioned motorbus
as their meeting place
their social hall
their respite from a heat wave
their temporary escape
from an impoverished life
without – perhaps –
any relief
in sight

Donald E. Allen

## A Handful of Wildflowers

I saw you in the park one day, and lost my heart in your blue,
blue eyes.
I asked you to a dance, and when you said yes, I knew I'd love
you … evermore.

I had no box of chocolates, no roses could I afford, but I had for
you a handful of wildflowers, as I knocked upon your door.

Our courtship was mostly innocent, long talks, quiet moonlight
strolls, shared dreams about tomorrow, and yet, dare I say at
times, our courtship was spiked with lust.

We kept our romantic dining simple, some cheese and bread,
some wine, oh, and wildflowers on the table were a must.

Your mom and three sisters sewed and sewed for months.  Never
had there been a more beautiful dress, never had there been a
more beautiful bride.

You had no expensive bride's bouquet, just a handful of
wildflowers; a symbol of our love as we stood there in the
presence of God, side by side.

Our babies all grew to call you Mother Dear. Johnny, Eric, and Paulette; she has my eyes and her mother's sweet, wonderful smile.

Paulette made it so very clear how much she loved us both when she carried a bouquet of wildflowers on her wedding day, as I walked her down the aisle.

Johnny went to Princeton, Eric … died in the war. We saved for years, and went to see that far away field where Eric left this earth. There in an endless rolling sea of green grass, a small patch of wildflowers grew.

We were drawn to them, across that hallowed ground, and when we reached those wildflowers we stood in silence and prayed. Don't ask how we were so sure this was the exact spot where Eric had died, Mother and I, just knew.

Now alone I climb the grassy knoll behind the church, as I have done so many times before. I'm much older now but I must go on; to your love I'm still a slave.

I'm out of breath while I seek your name among the silent stones. Of course, I carry a handful of wildflowers, to place upon your grave.

Linda Allocco

## Nightstand

Three-bedroom house, white shingles, faded black trim,
At the end of the block, over railroad tracks, two stop signs, and an
empty lot, overgrown with weeds,
The house down the gully, neighborhood kids would taunt.

Concrete driveway, paved the way to a narrow single car garage,
which no car could or would ever fit,
Filled with troves of rolling gadgets, rusted old seed spreader,
scraped bicycle, metal roller skates,
Leading to the stretched-out screen door, next to grey crusted crab
traps.

Inside, sagging mustard-colored cushioned couch faces the brown
bar, with peeling scratched laminate,
Circular stains, like snow globes, haphazardly decorate the
slightly tilted slab,
Two wooden stools, lean against the decorative faux brass
footrest.

Up the stairs, beyond the kitchen and the tiny salmon-colored
bathroom,
Down the hallway, with patched sheetrock, raised lumps, the size
of guarded fists,
A bedroom door, always closed.

On the other side, white dresser with scalloped mirror lines the back wall, filled with worn tiny flowered dresses,
Small bed, without a headboard, juts into the middle of the room,
Overflowing with soft stuffed well-tested friends.

Next to the bed, like a soldier standing guard, a gold-trimmed nightstand,
Single draw filled with a child's cherished treasures, found and protected,
Counted each night, like inmates housed behind bars.

Ten heart-shaped rocks, found in the dirt in the abandoned lot high above the gully,
Forty-seven years later, in the nightstand next to her bed, guarding her as she dreams,
Nine hearts remain.

## Sharon Anderson

### You Can Lead a Horse...

Forced by prompts and peer pressure,
I attempt to combine fragmented
thoughts and phrases,
but have no patience
with particles galloping about
the corridors of my mind--
open-backed ideas revealing
glimpses better left unseen,
ones bare of any meaning, or manners.

I pursue unrelated, overinflated
fancies that fly helium high,
concepts with no strings
attached, no way to snatch
their meaning--
they sail far beyond my reach.
My brain cries "foul,"
but those birds have flown,
leaving me without a feather in my cap.

The result of this expedition
into perdition, this rambling romp--
all pomp and no circumstance--
except for an overwhelming urge

to purge the whole and start anew,
lapping up inspiration
from a trough more familiar
where all thoughts are tightly tethered,
and all ducks, feathers intact,
are aligned neatly in a row.

# Rose Anzick

## Granddaughter

Your small, slender-fingered hand grasps my finger with vise-like strength.
The smile on your tiny mouth spreads sunshine, even in darkness.
Your trusting, eager face turns toward me for reassurance, of love?
I will always be there for you as long as I can.
The love I have for you is deeply ingrained.
My heart aches for you with fears and hopes for your future.
You are loved immeasurably.
No sunrise or sunset can compare with your beauty.
There is a gentleness and tenderness resilient in one so young.
The curiosity in you awakens my long sleeping memories.
It evokes pictures of my youth and makes me feel young and free again.
Joyfulness that you fill my heart with is ever present.
You are a tiny bundle of love that evokes so much emotion.
I carry a picture of you in my mind.

# Bob Baker

## Do You Want To Stay On The Path?

I had been on the path,
  For such a long long time;
    When I became aware,
      It was getting so late,
        Later with each passing hour;
          Darkness was fast setting in;
            And I had to change my direction;
            Cause I realized I lost my way.

          For so long I was on a course,
            Never deviating;
              Always going straight ahead,
                But now I felt so lost;
                  Didn't know whether to go back
                  Or keep forging on ahead;
                    My path was no longer clear,
                    And what to do, escaped me.

                  I didn't want to get more lost,
                    So I prayed for guidance;
                      Trying hard to determine,
                        Which was the right path for me;
                        Which I should now take
                        to find my salvation;

In time the answer I know
will be clear to me;
And so for now, I'll just wait,
Wait to see the light.

# Claudia Balthazar

## Deep

Love runs deeper than the ocean floor
I cannot see it, but I know it is there
Seeping through the abyss, slowly waiting to appear.
It is crushing, to know that love will come to this world in
any form –
It will rip through your frame and burst through your rib cage,
Burst blood through your veins and fill your heart up with rage.
Now wait...Love is a beautiful, magnificent thing –
Glitter and gold brightening up the scene and every little monster
in between.
Love stops your heart, it runs deep, I mean,
They say perception is reality though.
I looked at reality so –
I subliminally, slowly, deliberately, spread the cement around my
bleeding heart
and watch it dry into concrete.
I repair the cracks that appear every time you say the words that
are concrete.
How could I ever let you break me?
I ask every woman, when in love, is she weak?
Trembles and shivers, giggles and such.
Butterflies in my stomach. Every. Time. We. Touch.
Say we love each other.
Love just loves so surely, dies so sweetly, cuts so deeply…

Is love supposed to feel like this?

Am I supposed to always run from it?

I cry out, "Venus! Give me a man I could love forever!"

I want to love forever and be free,

But this "c'est la vie" thing caged my heart before it could learn
to sing!

Before I knew what unity was and way before I knew how to love.

So teach me

Teach me to never let go…

Make one, my body and soul.

Would it be beautiful if our souls intertwined the way our
bodies do?

And would it be beautiful if I meant it. Every. Single. Time. I said
I loved you?

Deep in the abyss slowly seeping through, I bury it before it
reveals itself to you.

How could I ever let you break me?

I ask a man, when in love, is he weak?

'Tis why every night I fight back the tears slowly rocking me
back to sleep.

And this too shall come to pass, is what a man once said to me.

# William Balzac

**Company**

There is no reason
For silence.
There is
No other thing on Earth
That ever arises
Without sound.
The World can embrace
A quiet place,
Where Love,
Is thought lost,
But found.

# Christine A. Barbour

## A Moss-filled Stone

Between classes,
under the blue spruce, I spend
time meditating on a rock we share
in a corner of the park,
quiet, green – the rock
worn out into a convenient
semi-circle that holds my behind
most comfortably.

Soon I see you
running towards me
over a moss-filled stone,
your flash of chestnut and
black stripe tail held up high,
not even an inch long,
as you flash by me,
your tiny ass exposed.
I could almost reach out
to touch your back; but,

you disappear up and over
the other side as your legs jump
into the air and land in the opposite direction
while I rest here contemplating

your fragile agility; and,
I wonder if you even saw me
sitting here waiting for you
holding my breath.

# Marilyn Barker

## Emotions...

Crammed inside of her
Like an over-stuffed trunk
Bursting at the seams
Until the hurt and pain
Ran out of her mouth
All over the party.

Feelings unfelt, denied
Shoved away
In dark recesses
Of body parts
Heartbeats
And memory banks.

Erupting
Unexpectedly
An over-heated volcano
Spewing hot emotions
Aimed at deserving targets
And some, maybe not.

Explosive words
Torpedoes unleashed
Uncontrolled rages

Flooding over tables
Knocking down wine bottles,
Flower vases and satin purses.

Replacing nonsensical chatter
With blood drained faces
The guilty and the not
Begging for escape
Back to hollow lives
Paved with whatever numbs.

# Antonio Bellia (Madly Loved)

## Expedition

It was so far
I had to fly,
I had to fly,
Very high to begin.

Very high,
Very
Far.

Then when my feet
Touched the ground
I thought I was
There.
I thought I could
Have got it.
I thought I could
Have grasped it
And run free.

But truly
I couldn't see
Too much mud,
Many walls,
Too many vines

Entangled me.

Elders' wisdom
Mothers' cries and Fathers' tries,
Mayors rich and
People poor,
Politicians shout
Politicians die
Sheepdogs kill sheep
Pigs made priests,

I just could
Not see.
Then I began
To search for
Me.
Yes, my flesh
Bled
My head
Fumed
My heart
Trembled.

Then a sparkle
I saw,
A gem.
It was me.
The sparkle became

A flash
So that I could
See.
Then I was
Free.

Cristina Bernich

**Upon the Night of the Waiting**

One final edit
useless,
as it is done.
Decided.
Future written, bound, and soon to be sold
to the most unwilling reader.
How odd to wait for news,
the publication,
the happenstance,
the fate of chance.
It is so unfathomable,
to think the discovery of a fated flaw,
un-erasable as it is,
will knowingly alter all future happenings, feelings,
the loves and lives of so many
forever and after.
Change the course
of everything.
The hearing of it, truly inconsequential, however,
as it is
done.
Bound by the Moirae.

Written and shelved in the stars,
years too late for revisions.
All there is
is the waiting of it.

# Thérèse M. Craine Bertsch

## Summer Camp

I feel the sunshine rays and view the pastoral scene
with clouds that dance across an azure sky
As pungent fragrance rises from our sweet earth
and roses sway secured upon the fence, their petals fly

A solitude engulfs this place,
with croaking frogs and fireflies
Here apple pie is recompense
for loneliness, and heartfelt sighs.

# Maggie Bloomfield

## Napping In the Rose Garden

Tired from your travails,
rest among these fragrant blooms,
Take respite from the pressure
of offices and oval rooms.

Sip this honeyed tea
to float away from strife and tears.
It brews a sweet siesta
for a peaceful hundred years.

Sleep, Sarah, sleep,
how spent your twisted brain must be,
Let chocolate ships invade your dreams
and carry you away to sea.

Ah, Michael, slumber,
while Mother sweetly sings,
and dream of unborn fetuses
that fly on tiny angel wings

Sleep, Mitchell, nestled
all warm within your tortoise shell.
In sleep those signs will disappear
consigning you to turtle hell.

Sleep, dear Kelly Anne,
upon denial's rose-red cloud
where broomsticks spark and splinter,
impale and burn the nasty crowd.

Dear Stephen, you yawn,
not used to being up at morn.
Your coffin opens in your dreams,
and little baby Steve's reborn.

Donald, your fingers
surely yearn to catch some zzzzzs
In dreams you'll build a Lego wall
that spans all earth, both lands and seas.

Warm in the sunshine,
free from worldly cares and fears,
mad roses blanketing your rest,
sleep on, dear fools, a hundred years.

# Carlo Frank Calo

## Back Home

The soldier stands, alone –
Back home! Life is normal and indifferent. There is no loss, no
burden, no mutual concern, no pain.
A bomb explodes in earshot; not a touch, not this time.
Back home! The debate is elsewhere. There are other problems to
discuss, needs which compete, issues to compare, priorities to
further assess.
The soldier kneels, alone –
Back home! A mother glances at an empty room, her baby – now
grown – far away. A sleepless wife reaches out with only the
pillow, cold and smooth, in response to her caress. A suitcase is
packed, the routine familiar, the call to duty – yet again –
expected. The goodbyes repeated but no less intense, with their
parting solitude, than the first.
A bomb explodes, now closer; the jarring, the jolt, is sensed.
Back home! The talk continues: elections and immigration, jobs
and taxes, guns and butter, Wall Street, Main Street, and – the
sanity, the safety, the sanctity – of "The Homeland." The chatter
on the cable, by the cooler, at the table, is preoccupied. The
politicos have other causes; the families, other concerns.
The soldier sits, alone –
Back home! Not so long ago much dialogue took place in the halls
of congress, on campuses, in the streets and on the news. Today,
there are neither victory gardens nor demonstrations. The children

of congress are not at risk. The campuses – bastions of thought – are safe, and silent.

A bomb explodes. It is not heard. It is not felt. It is not perceived at all.

Back home! A mother father sister brother husband wife son daughter partner lover friend: gather, in silence. They share one thing in common, a collective sacrifice, a word unknown to the rest of us who exist; unaware, uninvolved, unconcerned.

The soldier lies, alone –

Back Home...

Paula Camacho

**Letter My Grandmother Never Sent To Me**

I gave birth to thirteen children.
It is what we did in 1900
when there was no contraception or talk of it.
I was a farmer's wife producing workhands
like the cows and pigs that produced the food we ate
the grease for cooking collected from their innards,
too busy with wash and cleaning
to sit like a lady at tea.
I cut your aunt and uncle's hair
with a bowl on their head and sent them
to school in the same clothes every day.
Six of them died despite the good food I provided
pneumonia took most of them.
One day, diphtheria found its way into my flesh
killed my kidneys and me in mid-life.
Your mother being the oldest left school to take care of them
so if you find her controlling your aunts and uncle's lives
if you find her overbearing
if you find her controlling you
please find a way to understand.

# Loren Camberato

## Enlightenment's Dust

You are the end, the beginning,
and this moment, dissolved into the illusion of time.

An epiphany revealed to an opening of the mind,
offering vision toward the vast galaxy,
gazing from a dome perched alone at its knee.

As your marvel reaches the great night sky,
a humble exhale shoots roots to the earth from your thigh.

A murky pool is revealed at your toe,
blessing you to know as above is below.

Either way which you gaze,
you see the great depth of space
is your soul's reflection that you face.

A thought so great, your lungs reach deep,
its wind ignites a dormant seed.

The stars lean in to greet an old friend,
and times hand gently shifts the moon again.

# Lynne Cannon

## Awaiting Spring Tide

Oh, you dark-haired seductress
after the guests were gone

Taking to the sheets
like a surfer bolts to the waves

the rolling, pitching waves.

The bed still carries the scent
of rum and sweat
musk-sweet and tentative
as a virgin's touch.

A man was here last night
who made the voice dry
and the pulse and body ache;
the head aches as well.

Fair-eyed feline
with claws and sinuous limbs
that cling to a foreign body
after the sky has gone dark,
You shall know your heart when it
comes to you

drifting in on the tide,

on the last waves

It will come to you.

# Christina Canzoneri

## Snail In My Coffee

Found you today
Tiny life form perched on my coffee cup
Thought you were a speck of dust
So easy to crush you, to flush you
But you were beautiful
At second glance
A translucent spiral
Delicate as a baby's fingernail
Specks of brown around
Your shell delicately decorated
To entice a mate
At first
Thought to wash you away
Your spiral spinning down a whirlpool
But then I stopped…
Why did I need to kill you?
Maybe you were dead
Maybe you were not
Your visitation odd yet harmless…
Placed you on the aloe plant
Why end your journey with me
An unintended voyeur

Hours later you were gone…

# Kenny Carr

## Tinkerman

Tinkerman, say good man, sell me your wares,
your buffalo nickel, your freedom to roam,
your modesty, your majesty,
king of the open road.

Come sit a spell father and moisten your parch, sir.
Consider a barter before your departure,
–passing, leaving, no trust in a town–
my love for your rusted tin crown.

For there's new soles on your old brown loafers,
fresh tread for the hope drawn haul
and while there's still no time for running
I, too, shall heed the call.

Tinkerman, pray good man to the Lord, our God,
as cold hands lay, the last trump card;
Hearts expire, love endures.
For want of a savior, the Kingdom is yours.

# Mary Celeste

## True Romance

Romance is moments filled with small kindnesses
A kiss on the hand during a crowded party
Your hand on the small of my back
As you gently steer me through an open door

Arms wrapped around me in darkness
That keep me safe as I sleep
Your sweet breath upon my cheek
When sharing a blanket on the couch

Remember my birthday when you wore
My pink apron as you baked me a cake?
When did you forget how I like my tea?

Has it been so long since promises were made
In a church before God and hundreds of witnesses?
Words like love, honor, cherish and obey forever

When was the last time you gave me cards or flowers just
because?
Not because I'm angry at you or we argued over something trivial
True romance has slipped through your fingers
Like grains of sand in a delicate hourglass
That have fallen to the ground and washed away

I beg you to find it again
My heart yearns to make new memories
Of what once was me and you

# Caterina de Chirico

## Eleven Eleven

We're addicts, we're opium we're Vitamin C, we're opaque and translucent we're in bondage we're free, we're green eyes and brown eyes we're damaged and oh so sane, we're homeless we're barons we're warriors we're slaves. We're painters and poets we're hot and we're cold, we're angels and bitches we're Tristan we're Isolde. We're insatiable and dangerous, we're doctors and priests, we're infidels and mentors we're shamans and we're queens. We're Devas and Dakinis, we're vampires in the night, we're potent we're immortal, we're guardians of the light.

# Anne Coen

## Calligraphy Lesson

cap on head
glasses perched on nose
the calligrapher spoke:

here is bamboo,
popular subject in Chinese painting

bamboo has many qualities humans desire
bamboo must be strong,
yet flexible to survive

brushstroke same as making Chinese character
this is why we say we write painting, not draw

if you make mistake,
leave alone
cannot erase
sometimes you make worse
when you try to fix

mistake okay,
become part of design


smiling serenely,
he added,
life not perfect.

# Joseph Coen

## Against the Current

Winding the shifting turns of the dark night
I am one with the way ahead of me

Feeling the cold air on my bare arm
delighted that I am alive to sense it

Red luring lights pulling me ever onward
to an end I cannot see

I am one with the road
welcoming the harsh white light beating at me

I cannot stop
This is not the time
only dead bodies float with the current

Zach Gottehrer Cohen

**Reporters' Song**

We use the word "allegedly" to hedge
on capital-T Truths, from
lowercase spokesmen whose proofs
we find dubious.

Our keyboards clack
like drums of war, spies
and seasoned liars
around every corner

We are practiced hunters
of facts, tracking monstrous fictions
through suburban jungles,
stalking them off-the-record,
through the paper trail and
on deadline slay them
like Perseus with
a look in the mirror.

Quoting, "he said/
she said," we speak
with others' voices.
but we are not
voiceless.

We stand in the buffer zone
between warring mobs,
Mafioso politics and
pitchfork torches starved
for good news.

We are proxies for *vox
populi* because the powerful
take our calls.

We are looked to
to make sense of it all
we who, in the face of trauma
put down for the record all
but our own.

We who wander the obituary
graveyards, feigning grief, yet
feeling it deep, though different.

We dream in em-dashes,
to interrupt a muddy
thought with clarity, and flip
the world on its axis.

We question experts.
We know who knows.
We know who thinks
they know.

We know who wants us
to think they know.
We know who knows
we know they don't
but knows, in fairness,
we have to ask.

We expect answers.

When we interview
the Void, demanding,
"Why?"

We know better
than to accept its
vacant silence
in reply.

# Jamie Ann Colangelo

## Heaven Has a Dock

Heaven has a dock
It's my favorite place to go
There's no watching of a clock
Just the gentle waters flow

Surrounded by His peace
The warmth of the sun
Dancing rays of light
Creation stuns the Holy one

The scent of salted air
The breeze upon my neck
His touch runs through my hair
As I sit upon the deck

Drifting off to sleep
As the tide gently rocks
Cradled by His love
Here on Heaven's dock

# Anne Coltman

## Shadows

In silence she sits there
Blank stare behind a blank mind
Where am I, what has become of me
For my own self is hard to find

Then like the dimming of a light bulb
All goes dark before the surge
She contemplates in a squirt of recognition
Before in darkness she is again submerged

Then all at once the music starts
And the dance comes to mind
And the rhythm of those ankle bells
Renews the joy of days left behind

She's a dancer, a feather
That glides in potent will
Feet move, hands twirl
It's surreal because she's still

The tangled web that spews confusion
Leaves her speechless in its weave
So in her mind on she dances
Quite oblivious to folks who come or leave

A woman of talent, loving mother
Wife, sister and friend
Teacher of a dance that in her mind
Would never have to end

For in the waking of those tiring hours
When all seems lost
And her mind is just one big blur
She'll be glad to know again
This charming and lovable woman
For that's just how folks remember her

Though in silence she'll be seeking
For those loved ones she fails to recognize
Yet her heart knows they are near her
And in the shadows her heart sighs

Lorraine Conlin

**Triumph**

I followed Dad home from the Sportscar Salon
in his orange Plymouth Fury.
He drove my 1957 white TR3 convertible.

He zipped 'round cars and curves
weaving in and out of the fast lane.
Afraid to exceed the speed limit
it was hard to keep up with him.

He promised when we got home
he'd teach me how to drive the car,
a standard transmission which was all they had
when he was young and learned to drive.

He brought three bricks and a broken broom stick
into the kitchen, and told me to sit on a chair,
rest my feet flat on the floor and listen up.

I was shocked as I watched him lay the bricks
at the tip of my feet, spaced
exactly like the pedals in the new car.
*There, you have it. Clutch, brake, gas.*
*Grip the top of the stick and you're good to go.*

*Left brick, shift the stick into first gear*
*step on the right and ease up on the clutch.*
He repeated it, went through all four gears
the tricky reverse and sometimes he threw in the brake.

I tried, I really tried his prompts,
his litany of instructions and gestures.
I made the monotonous moves until my left leg cramped.
"This is stupid, Daddy, I'm getting nowhere.
Why can't we practice in the car like we did for my license?"

He said he'd decide when I was ready
for a real road test and then went to take a nap.

So it was back to the bricks,
side stepping and shifting gears
getting up from time to time to stretch my legs
until my brother came home and asked
if I was learning some crazy new dance.

When I showed him Dad's lesson plan
and executed the moves I was now good at,
he said, "Let's try it out in the car, I think you've got it."
Knowing Dad slept like a brick we took a chance.
After a few false starts and stalls,
lots of bucking and gear grinding
we made it off our block.

I felt proud making it up the hill into our driveway
stopped and put on the hand brake.

Dad came racing out of the house
waving the broom stick, yelling and
screaming that I disobeyed him.

He took away the keys, sent us into the house
put the top up on the convertible, snapped the window shut
and slammed the door.

I tried, complimenting his teaching methods,
saying he was a genius, the bricks and stick technique did
the trick.

He took me for his official road test
a week later, bought me a tank of gas.

He told me I was his best student.

# Jane Connelly

## Evening Vespers

We were speaking of the seasons changing –
The air cooler, the sun setting one minute
Earlier each night, when something
Made us both stop mid-sentence
Noticing the curve of Zach's Bay lit up gold.
The old concession building was glowing like a Greek temple;
It was the way the light drifted over the Comfort Station,
Bending around the corner, flowing out onto the landscape
That made us jump up, and run to see where the sun was
In the sky, yawning in the arms of the horizon.
We turned again and faced the Bay –
Musing on the sparkling blue water; the silent
Green wetlands reflecting against the blue.
Geese called out as they whistled over the roof,
Landing with a splash, and
We sat so quiet, so mesmerized –
We never even realized
Happiness had come to sit between us
For a spell.

Paula Curci

## Back at the Star-ship

I'm back at the star-ship again,
watching a tornado fire up in the night.
Little Big Town is harmonizing about the summer,
and I'm lost in the galaxy on a pontoon.

When we landed on this ocean highway,
in a red-hot wagon,
and made friends with Miranda,
no one questioned how we got here.

We are with all kinds of people,
swaying together with music as our vice.
Born and raised in Brooklyn matters none,
when these pistol packing bonfires start burning.

Cause blue grass burns
and rocks roll
no matter where you are from!

Max Dawson

**Human Technology**

Internet explorer, Gmail, Google Chrome
One's true love, millions of miles from their home
Instagram, Facebook, Snapchat and Twitter
Without at least one, your weird and maybe bitter
Social media, social networking a celebrity's internet shrine
Post someone else's private information online
iPads, iPods, cellphones galore
Utilized by those as little as 4
Computers, laptops, smartphones what's next?
Send the person sitting right next to you a text
On Demand, Netflix, and DVD Blu-ray
Xbox, Playstation, and Gamecube all day
Maps of earth from the view of a satellite
Internet surfing and World of Warcraft all night

# Kate Dellis-Stover

## The Miracle

She wrote hope.
Every word that fell into her diary was hope.
She was guided by angels.
Extraordinary angels
who offered her hope,
who kept her hope alive and strong.
She and her family lived quietly in a small apartment
while the world spun in black circles of evil
searching for just the right flesh to destroy.

Time crawled by slowly.
Too much time to think, to surrender to nightmares.
But Anne's nightly terrors disappeared with the soft light
of morning
or a gentle caress from her dear father.
She was young, but understood love
with the wisdom of an old soul.

Girls like Anne are beyond explanation.
They are willing to risk everything for the human heart and soul.
The light in their eyes speaks of something unearthly,
yet they celebrate trees and water and the shapes of clouds.

Even while the forces of evil threaten good people

who don't deserve to cower and hide
she writes hope.
She never stops writing hope.
She writes hope for others,
she writes hope for herself
and even if darkness consumes her,
she does not die.
Her heart and soul shine like a beacon
to show others the way,
the way to persist
the way to have faith, the way to keep faith against all odds,
the way to look past a seething, dark heart
and see something else,
something distant but unmistakably human.

Where are the monsters?
Do they follow us, do they haunt us?
What about the monsters?
They plead with us, they weep, they stretch out their hands
to touch us.
Please, please see past my ugliness.
I know I am large and awkward.
But imagine for a moment my heart.
Love is what I need just as you need love.
Is it asking so much?
Do you want me to go back to the streets alone?
We are more alike than you think.

Anne would not hesitate to take the clawed hand of the beast.
She would look into its eyes tenderly,

she would sit with her arm around it while it cried.

The beast would know, with such gratitude, that she had no fear.

No fear. Only love.

A love without limits.

A love of such magnitude that it lived in her small body

without a hint of judgment.


I pray to be closer to her, to be more like her.

I hope her spirit surrounds me and guides me.

Yes. The world is too much with us, late and soon.

She knew. She knew this.

That didn't stop the miracle that fell from her small, white hands.

# M. A. Dennis

## Junk Food Junkie

I woke up with morning sickness
It was something I ate last night
For the past few 365 days
I've been feeling sick
It could be the pesticides
Or the high blood sugar syrup
Making me licensed to ill
How do I soothe my savage Beastie?
Boys like me go coo-coo
For co-co-dependency:
Processed food and I, need each other
What a conun-drumstick!
Everything I love to eat makes me sick:
W-T-F-sick, S-M-H-sick
I-D-K-what to do-sick
Artificial ingredients insult my intelligence
Too many empty calories
Have left me stuffed with angst
I need to take a re-laxative
Make a movement
Toward better health
While weighing the pros and con-
stipation of "Start on Monday"
Procrastination

Prometheus stole my fiery spirit
Self-control is a myth
Consuming mass quantities
Of too much sugar is real

Fake news is easier to swallow
Than this red pill realization:
I'm perpetuating a vicious cycle,
Going through the same dietary motions
But expecting different (results may vary)
Jesus, Joseph and Mary
Is Christianity gluten-free?
If so, put me on the church's shut-in list
Because I'm sick, a junk food junkie
Craving a fix
Withdrawal symptoms got me feeling
Ugh, Yuck, Ick—from going cold turkey
(instead of hot bacon)
I'm sick to my stomach
From what I put in my stomach
My belly has fat more dangerous than
Being trapped in Hippo-crates
Let self-poisoning be thy medicine:
Pick your food
That's the lesser of this or that
Decisions, decisions, decisions
Whole grain organic, versus
Cryogenically preserved
With preservatives
My vital organs cry out: GO VEGAN

Stop eating things
Made with things you can't pronounce
Subtract from your diet
Anything nutritionally amounting to nothing
Anything with additives added
Until it equals No Refrigeration Needed
I need a drink...something green
So I can detox, while waving the white flag

Yet, I refuse to throw in the white flour
There's something sour
About diet drink sweeteners
But I continue nursing my bliss
Ignorance comes in many colors:
Red #40, Yellow #5; mix them together
And you get a soda that rhymes with orange
Something to wash down my little Blue #1
Disclaimer: If my eating binge should last
Longer than a four-hour-erection
Don't call the doctor
Instead, prop up the pillows on my deathbed
Because I'm dope sick and I'm trying to kick
Even if it kills me...

David Dickman

## It Won't Be Long

It won't be long
Ere I walk again
Where I've walked so long before

Be it city street or mountain trail
Or lonely country lane
I take them in with a rhythmic tramp
Giving melody to the way.

It won't be long
Ere I think of thoughts
I'd best not have thought at all

Of songs and twirls of luscious curls
And frosty turquoise dawns
I bring them back "big as life"
Getting lost in dreamy ways.

It won't be long
Ere I try to learn
What I've tried to learn before

I strive to plan for later life
So losing hold on youth
I am pained as it tears away
So I walk my dreamy lanes.

It won't be long
Ere I've lived out life
Feeling I've done nothing at all

Walking those wasted whiles away
With thoughts tied up in curls
Mem'ries of visions of could-have-been
Blotting out what I've done.

# Linda Trott Dickman

## Just Beyond Wit's End
*For those who tie knots*

Just beyond Wit's End,
there is a garden,
the wildflowers are safe,
the lawn is just perfect
for laying back, lacing fingers.

The paths are lined in pine
soft needles cushioning tired feet.
Logs burnished by many winters
joined together to comfort.
The chimney boasts an oak fire,
a hint of orange in the air.
Whiffs of maple syrup, pancakes and bacon beckon.

Just beyond Wit's End, the door is open,
seating mismatched, comfortable,
beverages warm the hand, the moments,
bouquets hued in autumn console.

There are knot tying classes, taught
by a Shepherd who knows how
to tend to the rope burns,
frayed ends, tired arms, burdened souls.

The soundtrack soothes and the pain
pushes out like a splinter.
The words come, finding their way
to paper, conversation, prayer.
There is the scent of balsam fir
issuing from the pillows.

Just beyond Wit's End, the atmosphere
assuasive, the conversation lifts,
the silence, burnished.
Sputtering wicks given air, cockles warmed.

At Wits End, the cups
are filled with kindness.
The only drink that is served, lives.

# Anthony DiMatteo

## Nukes vs. Zombies

Progress today – my twelve-year old
admitted he was more afraid of nukes
than zombies – a distinction comparable
to state and church who fight over the body
and soul of the living and the dead.

I tell him how we'd hide under desks.
Twice a year, a siren would sound.
Hands over head like embryos
in a jar, we'd jam ourselves down,
turtles praying against extinction.

"Dad, what if zombies got the nuke code?"
I put my hand to my head and laugh.
Science and religion have shaken hands
in his mind despite a brief respite.
We dream things up more than we know.

Each generation gets to imagine
the end of things in its own fashion.

# Susan Grathwohl Dingle

## An Explanation

i

The reason it seems like the world is falling apart
is because it really is,
just look at that desk.
The souvenir fairies from Ireland, gift from your granddaughter,
still in cellophane, next to the textbook
of Alcoholics Anonymous on top of
new and selected poems that explain about God,
the timesheet for the caregivers whose shifts
begin today, after the Primary Care
Physician said you are failing.

You disagree. You think there is a new injection
the doctor doesn't know about. In your sleep you explain.

I catalog what is falling apart. So far
I didn't even finish
the desk. Finally the handmade wooden manger scene
is in order, the interlocking pieces
grooved together, the hooves of the camel
on top of the hooves of the lamb, and the human
curves stacking neatly around them.
It took me twenty minutes to put it back together,
without the diagram I couldn't find

until I didn't need it any more.

ii
No one starts out being a hoarder.
It's just when you lose so much,
you can't let anything go. Hence, old Christmas cards
that returned in the mail
from people who are probably dead
or they moved, you can't keep up with them;
canvas bags filled with magazines whose unread
articles might matter someday;
papers you can't think of where to file,

a souvenir bottle in the shape of a maple leaf
filled with syrup, from a wedding in Vermont
(the handmade tag says "Thank You,")
a heart constructed of Legos by a granddaughter several years ago,
and a plastic dog the size of a fingertip another granddaughter
gave me as I was leaving,
"something to remember her by."

I dream of clear surfaces,
where all the old clothes have been given away
and a homeless woman is enjoying
sewing on the button for that cable knit sweater
I can no longer wear.

iii
God is good, forever giving us things to do
when we think we should be doing

something else, for example
paying bills right now,
especially the electric,
three months overdue, because you
were always on top of such things,
your ledgers now illegible,
handwriting cramped into hieroglyph
letters like ibis scratching across Egypt.

I am color-coding folders,
red is for Home Care, green is for
Caregiver Schedules, purple is for Poems (Current.)

On the desk I find a yellow plastic
tape measure labeled "For help with blindness,
please call National Federation for the blind."

iv
Anything made of cloth
can be folded, and placed in a pile.
Then the pile can be moved to a different room.

v
I wish I knew what to do with books I haven't read
or how to repair the nightstand
that shattered in the bedroom the last time you fell.

# Sharon Dockweiler

## Open Mic

I wrap my hand around the open mic,
my old friend before a sea of strangers' faces.
Teetering on the edge of the room's expectations,
I am back in my element.
With a confident wink, I begin.

No introduction.
My words speak for themselves.
My volume grabs.
My whispers invite.
My timbre seduces.

I ride the wave of responses,
the "mm-hmm"s and "That's right!"s,
all the way to the applause.

On my way back to my seat,
I get wide-eyed whispers of "Awesome!"
I settle back, savoring, sated,
haughtily thinking,
"Top that!"

I pull the reins on my runaway thoughts
to focus politely on the next poet.

I'm sure they won't do as well as I.

I am wrong.

So very. Very. Very. Wrong.

Poets, singers, performers, one after another, take the stage.
Some touch me so deeply,
I want to etch their words on river rocks
and hold them inside my mouth.

One man, standing in a corner all evening
until the host cajoled him into sitting at the keyboard.
If ever I had a child,
I would have wished this man to sit beside her crib each night
to sing and play her lullabies.

A girl got up, young Twenty's, not quite cooked yet, carrying
a guitar.
She had majored in music in college, but lost the will to play
soon after.
Recently, in the hope that she is healing, friends bought her
this guitar.

"I'd like to play a song for you," she said,
"But I'm not ready yet.
But here's my guitar.
Her name is Clarice.
Say hello to Clarice."

"HI, CLARICE!"
She sat.

*That's it?*
*She's not playing a song?*
*But...*
*But...*
*But...*
*That's...*

*BRILLIANT!!!!*

She's daring to refuse to pretend she is well when she is not.
She will not bow simply to ensure that others will not feel uncomfortable.

Loving someone who is ill *is* uncomfortable.
We sick ones cannot lift our beds and walk again to spare our loved one's pain.

Thank you, oh, thank you, O not-quite-cooked-yet, very depressed,
Twenty-something.
You, tonight, are the lighthouse on the shore
for this fifty-plus year-old heavyweight prizefighter-of-depression
who,
after forty-four years of suicidal ideation,
just two months ago,
in a perfect storm of calamity...

      was brought down by the enormity of our common illness.

I came to hear you straight from a doctor
who informed me just how badly she thinks I may have injured
myself internally.

Before this office visit, I had been feeling the best I have since my attempt.
I arrived at the open mic angry at the world.

But I do not have the luxury of anger.

That knowledge is wisdom worthy of gratitude.
It brings me to God…and often to open mics.

I left that gathering taken down a peg, but lifted up several,
having been useful, loved and edified.

Open mics are powerful.
When performers are honest, and brave,
We connect.
We surgically drain the poison from our wounds
and knit ourselves
back to life.

# Terryl Donovan

## My Hands are Empty

My hands are empty.
I have put aside my work
to dwell on the possibilities
of birdsong and whalesong,
their melodies celebrating wonder.
I sit in the dark, alone.
Watching the night sky,
comet streaking in the distance,
stars and moons stroking
the invisible clouds in the dark.
The light from the night sky falls
on my open hands,
urging them to keep still,
to notice the possibilities hiding
in the invisible cloud of my mind.

# William Doyle

## Casus Belli

Lie, beat, bash, repeat
Are we not what we defeat?
Lest not we hold ourselves to this,
Else we only spawn more red mist.
Denounce and defame,
Plunge deep the athame;
Into their men and our children
Until we have killed a billion--
Nay more we seek and crave,
For we make each one brave.
The wars we fight are all the same,
And yet we always shift the blame.
Temporary remains always the gain
Whilst both parties sit silent in pain.
We have pledged: "Never Again"
And "Lest We Forget," Amen.
Yet we break this prayer,
None too rare.

We, the creatures of habit,
Kill each other in endless cycle.
And in all that we inhabit,
We surely do recycle--
Our blood, our bodies, to this earth.

Our constant justifications,
They provide a solace and bit of mirth,
So that we may doom more generations.

Each Casus Belli we use,
Render the next one easier to make.

# Peter V. Dugan

## Open Mic at The Oswego Tea House

Rock-hopper Koala
a showboat showoff,
one of the real neophyte off-white
hot pants flappers.

Dances in an itsy-bitsy glitter
glass bikini
with the body of a brass wine flask,
suffers peg-leg stigmata,
recites sonnet texts from a silo oracle.

The accompanist Bristol Esau
(a snooker table pen name)
and a member of the royal society
of radio cyborgs,
tickles the Tibetan Ivories,
performing unicorn boogie-woogie,
an operatic euphony
on a withered out of tune
stuntman organ.

Together they open woe,
open wounds, peel away
scabby scars of society,

impale inanimate lunar moths
with needles of pliable tantric
marsh mellow melodies,

Odd asps of modern art
highlighted in a toga opine annex.
Music and verse presented
in a nanobot nutshell,
spiced with nutmeg,
saved by hell's bells.

# Ronald Edwards

## Out on the Limb

In the corner
of a yard
there stands a tired old tree.

No leaves, no fruit,
the branches scarce.
Sap flows but just barely.

Scrub brush growing
with some weeds,
vines are on the trunk.

Litter thrown
about its plot,
strewn with discarded junk.

Laughter lost
within the wind,
broken swing holds still.

No longer found
down on the ground
Blue Jays or Whippoorwill.

Boughs once strong
with foliage green
did shield the mighty sun.

Providing shade
about the glade
for children having fun.

Days of grandeur
long since gone,
a cord soon to become.

Cast iron hearth,
black arms of girth,
hot ambers will succumb.

Was it by chance
upon the day
when woodman's ax drew near,

that wind did blow,
thrashed to and fro,
deadwood broke free and clear?

As if a surgeon's
skillful hand
had pruned away the chaff.

Did needed sculpture
cutting deep,

left standing merely half?

Heavens parted
with beams of light,
a genesis began.

Possibilities emerged
like sprouts
in planters pan.

From once what was
a lifeless growth,
new hope began to brim.

Blossomed forth
fresh fruit and leaves
now found out on the limb.

# Alex Edwards-Boudrez

## Retreat From Aging

Twenty-plus years ago
I mounted a magnifying mirror
So my brave wife could step
Outside of herself
And examine the truth
That is her privilege to alter
Each day.

Today
I finally took a dare
And took a good long stare
At myself.  I suffered
A bruising voice
That pulled no punches:

"Oh my!  What has become of you?
The way you look is way beyond repair!
Potholes in the crumbled concrete,
Mounds of loamy sand
Sprouting gray seedlings of sagebrush
On ridges of parched red rock formations."

"Wow," I offered, "You have a way with words."

"There's more. Lean in closer,
Closer still; be still and gaze
At all that your delusion obscures."

"Is that distortion really me?"

"It's not a distortion.
It's my re-creation
Of your raw perfection."

The mirror fell silent,
Hanging there, implacable,
Framing landscapes of craters,
Dunes, depressions, lakes
Spilling over silted clumps
Around the mouths of caves
Under a crooked bridge.

Rolling over this foreign terrain,
The echo of a familiar troll:
"Linger no longer or you'll be gobbled up!
I'm here to set your fear in motion
For your salvation.
Step back inside your head,
Forsake the truth, cast courage aside,
Be happy with your fantasy feast
Of canned preserves inside your opaque jar."

# Joanne Esposito

## Darkness to Light

Darkness, Stillness, Quiet, Evening
Thanking Jesus for the day
Forgive me when I stray

Problems can stand tall in the dark
I place them in your hands Jesus
Darkness becomes Holy
There are treasures there

A bird sings in the darkness of a storm
A mustard seed of faith
I surrender, what's the answer

Like the sun peaks the dawn
Jesus Light breaks through
He is here in this storm
My heart has hope

Be Still! He is my Father
I am His child!
I can talk to Him!
His love is Brighter than the sun

Jesus spoke
I am the Light of the World.
Whoever follows me
will not walk in darkness
(John 8:12)

# Jack Farrington

## The Picture Show

Many tangled webs of misery--but
my brain-- it does not see
fleeting shadows and dancing figures
within a darkened canopy.

Round and round full it goes
figures that cling to me
dart and dance and sing such things
but still-- my brain can't see
my heart it knows it knows too well
these things that are not right

for it shakes and quivers and bellows heed
the terrors of the night
dreams within, dreams without, my heart
it doesn't know
my brain which schemes and scams about
holds me captive to a picture show.

# Kerry Fastenau

## Mortal Guise

I watch you dance for the tourists
Under the half-drunk eye of Bacchus
Fixed between beats of *Hasapiko*
Your legs strong as carved marble

In the half-lit taverna, your profile
Seems conceived by a master sculptor
Your balanced mouth ambiguous,
Your brows furrowed, concentrating

The dancers in a line, arms entwined
Hand upon shoulder--draped--
Yours are perfectly carved
I imagine their weight upon me
The *domestica*, sanguine in a glass,
Warming the blood in my veins
I draw in another mouthful, swallow,
And think of the taste of your lips

Later, after I know you are mortal,
I still feel the wine flood my veins
And the music pulse through me
At the contemplation of your thighs.

# Carlita Field-Hernandez

## Vines

Do you remember how when you're little
The back of your mother's legs
Was the safest place in the world?
Burying your face in the cloth of her pants
Somehow cured shyness, anxiety, and pain.
I get the same feeling
From the spot between his jaw and shoulder
Nuzzled against his neck.

As I breathed him in
His pulse against my cheek
Softly
And lazily
Peppering his warm,
sweet,
skin
With kisses
Like teardrops
I knew it may be for the last time.

He breathed out
And along with his breath
He carried three words
That I so longed to hear

When we were apart
Barely comprehendible

Pulling my head out of its safe place
So I could listen more closely
"I've missed you"
His strong arms tightened around me
Faceting me to him
To the point that it seemed as if
We had always been this way.

My words came out small
Barely above a whisper
Afraid of any disruption
To such a perfect moment
"I love you"

Two warm
Wet
Lips
Pressed against my forehead
So fast
But soft
And calculated
1...
2...
3...
His head rolled back onto the pillow
"I love you too"

We had closed the garden to our hearts
And prepared ourselves to never look back
But the flowers still bloomed
The ivy still crawled
And much like our love
Was a wild
Untamable force
Still beating
And thriving
Even though we had walked away.

But wild flowers are tricky
And when gardens grow rampant
The thorns do too
And just when I thought
I was ok with saying goodbye
It ensnared me
The vines coiled
Around my arms and legs
Cementing me there
Forcing me to face
All I was leaving behind
And so I screamed for help
But only flowers fell from my mouth

My beautiful garden
Our beautiful memories
Became my captor
My limbs grew weak
As the vines that fed off the memories we shared

Pinned me to the ground
I beckoned for you to come back
I dreamt that you would come back
A dream where my face never left the security of that spot
between your jaw and shoulder.

But when we said goodbye
When we said I love you
When I slept with your arms tightly around me
You did not feel the pull of the vines
Like me

# Melissa E. Filippelli

## The Softest Kind

Time
like a quiet professor
never rushed
always there
constant in its attention.
The Weaver
of a great many things
of quality and substance and depth.
Patience
being one of the greatest lessons
time has the ability to teach
gifts us with
an increasing knowledge and ability
to surrender to the Greater and
how to be content in what is
not what could be.
"Killing me softly"
comes to mind.
Time is a killer
of the softest kind.
Grace
takes its time
showing us our abundance and our lack---
where we must be grateful

where we must improve.
Over time
time teaches us, really
what living actually means---
how to breathe
how to bleed
how to love and
not to waste
what we've been so generously given
Time.

# Adam D. Fisher

## In The Fall Forest
(Five haiku and a tanka)

1.
A deep layer of
oak, sassafras, poplar leaves
clothe the forest floor.

2.
Red, yellow, brown leaves
floating in a forest stream
become vibrant-bright.

3.
White leaves on black pond
where swans float, startlingly white,
on this dark gray day.

4.
Bright green on a rock
neither spread fabric nor tarp—
lush green late fall moss.

5.
Red/orange fungi,
some clusters, others have rings
grow on a black birch.

6.
White lichens like the
top of a Corinthian
column grow out of
an oak's deep wound eight feet high,
but sap still flows under bark.

# Kate Fox

## You Should Be Here
*for Eileen and Jeannie*

Feeling alone
In a room full
Of people
I wonder if
You hear the
Music I'm
Sharing in
My Heart

Anytime I
Walk into
Another place
I am overwhelmed
By the
Empty space
Your absence
Leaves in me
Always hoping
The din will
Dull the pain

I move forward
Even as you're

Slowed
The guilt I feel
Overshadows
My steps

Feeling alone
In a room full
Of people
I wonder if
You hear the
Music I'm
Sharing in
My Heart

# Grace Freedman

## To My Husband
### September 12, 1945

I miss you, I've said it a hundred times or more
Since that unforgettable day, when you marched off to war.
I miss you, can these three simple words convey
The heartbreaking anguish suffered by your going away.

The days were long, but the nights were more trying
On my nerves, and most of them were spent crying,
But I prayed, too, I prayed to the good Lord above
To keep you safe and sound, bring you back soon to your love.

There were days when your wonderful letters came
Days that were set apart, because they were not the same
As when there was no mail from "my only one"
And on those days for me there was no sun.

And then those terrible, terrifying weeks of waiting
For letters that did not come, no word, my hope fading,
Until one day a telegram carried its message of good news,
You were safe, slightly wounded; it chased away my blues.

Words cannot express my relief
My only outlet for all the grief,
All those pent-up tears soon fell,

For the one I love so well.

And now, though much time has lapsed with fear
That long awaited, wonderful day is drawing near
The day when my love will again be here
We'll be joined in all we both hold dear.

And so, my darling, I am trying to express,
How you alone can bring much happiness
How much you mean to me always
I look forward to the rest of our days.

# Glenn P. Garamella

## Second Wind

Formed from clay, we appear a mannequin to humanity;
the voice inside the shell, searching the beach for the sound of
the ocean.

Tired of living a half-life, we are slow in our appreciation of
the world, slower still
for our love of it.

Keeping our neighbors at arm's length, kicking at the dog and
the day.

We watch from separate windows wearing our bodies like
ill-fitting clothes.

Half baked, like the bread which refuses to rise.

We know our age as we turn the dates on cans of expired food.

Some of us see the glass half full, others do not see the glass at all.

We wait for a second wind to sweep us off our feet and slowly
breathe us back
to life and to our senses.

# M. Francis Garcia

## Bowing Out

Branches lean forward
as daylight quickly fades;
tomorrow April arrives
wearing blue woolen cape
to fight early spring chill
around the narrow nape
of her neck.

# G. S. George

## The Poem You Never Wrote

The poem you never wrote lies
in a drawer on a blank page.

On quiet mornings, your eyes still closed,
you think you can hear its faint call.
Like a song written in invisible ink
it waits to appear perfect and whole.

Were your seminal words too weak
for your thoughts to be conceived,
like the children you never had
because you did not have the means?

Or perhaps you felt the silence was more
worthy than any sound you might impose
on a world that's seen and heard too many words.

Whatever the cause, its moment has passed,
and soon your poem will join all regrets
that lie beneath time's eternal ocean.

# Tina Lechner Gibbons

## Stage Struck

My mother wanted me to be a doctor,
I wanted to be an actress.
She used to call me Sarah Heartburn,
but I wanted to be Deborah Kerr
dancing the polka with Yul Brynner.
I grew up to be neither…
Or maybe…
At the age of 10
I won a polka contest
wearing my mother's wedding dress as
my costume.
I've bandaged cut fingers and
kissed a few boo boos away,
I've mended broken hearts,
but not my own,
doctors cannot heal themselves.
Then came the time I didn't get to be
Deborah Kerr,
I got to be Yul Brynner –
I survived,
and
every day I act.
I act like everything is normal.
I've become adept at applying the smile

to my face,
and reading the script.
The script that ends happily ever after,
until it all goes dark,
the audience has gone home,
and I am left alone
on the stage.
No applause,
no encore.

# Shilpi Goenka

## The Trap of Eyelashes

Why do women want
so desperately, to extend
the mesh of
their eyelashes,
add fake ones, and
use bold mascaras.
Aren't those flashy,
dense and complicated,
deceptive piece of few eyelashes,
enough to confuse a man already?
Like a *Venus flytrap,*
they open and close,
the prey captured and
digested inside.
Tell her–
boldness comes from
the simplicity of one pure
intention and,
extending her heart
instead.

# Jessica Goody

## Words and Music

Rain drums the windowpanes like percussion
as the storm crescendos, the glass streaming.
Such a day calls for jazz. Ella's tongue-twisting
scat reminds me of the precision of language,

experiments with sound, rhythm and syllable.
I tap my pencil in time to her crooning strain,
pondering "Lionel Hampton's instrument": ten
letters, starts with V. My pencil stutters against

the tabletop, keeping time as I count the spaces,
testing each letter to see whether the potential
combination makes a word. With each completed
clue, another cross-street appears on the grid,

the black and white squares stark as sheet music.
The last note hangs in the air; the last blank white
space waits to be filled, a single vowel making the
difference between gibberish and a genuine word.

# G. Gordon

## The Eyes of Rita Monte

The eyes of Rita Monte
have seen the love of a friend
These soulful eyes have given love to a mother
husband and son
The eyes of Rita have seen loss and heartache.
These eyes live to tell the story of strength and compassion.
These eyes are the most faithful
the world can hold as they worship a saint like
Padre Pio.

The eyes of Rita Monte
are indeed not common nor ordinary
they cannot be explained.
They are an enigma
that holds the mysteries of beauty
forevermore.
These are the eyes of Rita Monte
and I know them well.

# Aaron Griffin

## Bluebell Railway

May had come.

In a matter of weeks, flowers would bloom in the Bluebell Valley.

The little maintenance diesel did its part to keep the tracks through the Valley straight and sturdy.

But without a train to carry visitors, no one would come to see the flowers.

And for a flower-viewing train, a dull diesel wouldn't do.

They would need a special engine, they would need the magic of steam.

A Bluebell Engine – could one still exist?

The Driver and Mechanic of the tiny diesel, No. 5, their lunch-pails packed for a long journey, boarded their engine, and set off.

Across the viaduct spanning the vast gorge in the morning,

Through cluttered depots where trains large and small jostled for passage as the sun set,

And through the city at dusk, where clusters of moths orbited street lights, as the windows of town houses went dark.

Deep in that city, in the moon-cast shadows of steel-mills and cement plants, was spread the lonely train graveyard.

No. 5 rolled silently in between stacks of decrepit coaches, half-dismantled frames of formerly proud express engines, the rusted-out boilers of little shunting locos, and lines of coal tenders which had long ago lost their engines to the cutter's torch.

Freight cars piled high with old wheels, dismembered boilers and other random parts, were arranged in long rows that stretched into the shadows.

Rats scurried about the scrapped remains of engine cabs, still serving as shelters even with no train crews to huddle under them.

Water dripped everywhere, though it wasn't raining. Decaying steel groaned under the stress of its own weight.

The steam age came here to die.

And the shed where the old engines were kept was now only full of dismantled parts.

But against all odds, on a side track, hidden behind the rusted-out hulk of a much larger locomotive, was a little tank engine with a tall funnel.

It was dirty, but not rusty at all. It had all six wheels, its boiler and smokebox were in place, there was coal in the bunker.

And to the surprise of the crew of No. 5, an old man, wrapped in his blanket in the spring night air, stood in the cab, a thermos of hot tea in his hands.

"This is No. 55, my old engine." He said. "We called her 'Stepney' back in the good old days. She'll be broken up for scrap soon, so I came to say goodbye."

"Well goodbye can come later." Said the little diesel's driver. "We need an engine for our line in the Bluebell Valley, and this one here is perfect!"

And the heist began.

Stepney's driver found a hose and filled the water tanks, and No. 5's mechanic lit the fire and began shoveling coal, all while keeping as quiet as they could.

Several tense hours later, the little engine was in steam, and the crews of the two locomotives guided their machines stealthfully (or as stealthfully as two industrial conveyances could be) out of the scrapyard, through the city, and back onto the rails of their own safe railway.

The fugitive engine arrived at the valley to a big welcome of all the townspeople.

The Bluebell Railway had its first engine, and with some paint, polish, and oil, Stepney was ready to help all the passengers who came to visit during bluebell season, and as the years went on, it became a haven for all the escaped steam engines that were saved by —

"Aaron, turn off that Thomas tape and get ready for dinner!"

shouted my mother.

"Yes Mom!"

I sat at the dinner table bouncing in my chair.

I didn't know yet that the Bluebell Railway wasn't just a fairy tale, and that twenty years later I'd be booking a flight to a town in England my travel agent never heard of, all so I could ride slow old trains with no air conditioning, and take selfies with Stepney's engine friends like Baxter, and Bluebell, and Adams.

But I was six then. And the fantasy of a magical railway that ran through a valley of bluebells where escaped steam engines pulled old wooden carriages full of visitors would be enough for me.

I never got to pilot the Megazord, attend Hogwarts, or become a Pokémon Trainer.

But did spend a week traveling up and down the Bluebell Railway.

And with that memory in my heart, I navigate my society's rigged, dystopian economy, still believing that my other dreams may still come true.

# George Guida

## Safe, Quick Vasectomy!

How Sharp are a Gator's Teeth?

The woman you met online last week
reads the billboards and gives directions
to the roadside Citrus Travel Center
where you can read the pamphlet
and watch the baby reptiles sun
while munching a hunk of pecan brittle
en route to a Florida beach motel.

# Maureen Hadzick-Spisak

## Piano Baby

Every Sunday she sat
Her legs dangling, swinging slightly
To the soft music.
Her eyes wide, staring
Not at the piano, but
The doll that sat on top.
She longed to pick it up
Untie the white eyelet bonnet
Touch the blonde bisque curls
Even kiss its up-turned nose.
The doll seemed to crawl toward the music
Kicking one foot into the air
The lace of her bloomers peeking out
From under her peach dress.
Her intaglio blue eyes
Beckoned Sarah across the room.
As she reached the piano
Her mother's voice sang out
*Look, but do not touch.*

# Geneva Hagar

## Atlas Held Up the Heavens

So many moons of
        almost daylight pass
when workers pause
        to wipe their brow.

I hear their haunting cries
        puckering the sky
like needle pricks
        that numb the pain.

In thick-sole boots they labor
        in solemn weather toil
an army of the faceless
        unnoticed by the world.

# Nick Hale

## Beachhead

There is no forest here,
 no trees.
They say the wind is too
strong for them to grow.
There is no mountain god here
to sacrifice
innocence and despair.
We are the mountains here.
The waves bow down
in reverence
to our chalky crags.
Every prayer takes a little
more from us.

There are no trees here
to swing from like a
grisly pendulum,
no signpost reminding you
you are not alone.
No evidence of those
who came before
dashed at our feet,
swallowed by the sea.

# Robert L. Harrison

## Victim

He was convinced the mirror
was bought from some amusement park
for it made him look heavy and his
face would make a ghost smile.
So he moved closer and gained ten pounds
then lost it as he backed away.
He turned around quickly as if to see
if his image changed or if
the mirror would lie again.
And with his breath he fogged it up
to hide reality,
but after wiping it clean
his body was clear to see,
a victim of all the years
of not believing in mirrors.

# Gladys Henderson

## The Lesson

When I was in art school,
the professor taught us
to look at the space between,

the air around each object,
not the *object*.  He called it,
*negative space*.  So I look

today at tree branches,
air that rubs up against
their barks, scarred limbs;

think of what I could have said
to you but did not, my voice
stunned, the disappointment

too new, the wound so deep
it went to my heartwood.  Silence
was better, *negative voice* I'll call it,

in memory of my professor.

# Judith Lee Herbert

## Magician

Instead of holding onto grace tightly,
the way I cherish the garnet ring from my sixteenth birthday,
I want to hold grace as gently as
the painting of bamboo and snow in pale moonlight
floats in a silver frame in my hallway.

Instead of holding onto joy tightly,
the way I save old hallmark cards from people I love,
bound with rubber bands on a shelf in my closet,
I want to hold joy deeply, the way
the ocean sustains abundant life
that thrives unseen in the depths below.

Instead of holding onto grief tightly,
the way I cling to black and white photos of those
who came before me, I want to hold grief lightly,
the way a magician shrouds his white dove
in blackness inside a top hat, feels its wings flap,
and releases it into brief timeless flight,
knowing it will return.

# Sheila Hoffenberg

## Do Not Awaken Me

I'm in another world that's hard to understand
A message that is whispered softly
Sounds emerge, a voice remembered
As your face appears as once it was
Mesmerized, confused, elated and bizarre
Words that enchant but cannot be described
You look at me, but the expression is not clear
My body is still, my eyes in REM
Where am I? I wonder, but no one hears
I reach to touch you, but you fade away
Is it just a mirage, a vision, I can't decipher
My heart is pounding, my mind's in a whirl
So much to apprehend as my thoughts revolve
I know that it was you, but you are gone

I don't want to awaken but reality takes over

As I lay there alone with memories to keep me company

# Arnold Hollander

## are we saving time?

are we saving time?
some say that we
are really wasting time
moving clocks ahead then back
in early spring and late fall.

I wonder if the crocus
notices a clock hand
reversing itself or a robin
awakening an hour later.

time is a construct, an idea
that establishes a method
for us to mark the moments
between dark and light.

nature has its own clock
it also uses the sun in either

a full bright display or
hidden as the earth rotates
on its axis and at the same time
revolves around the sun.

perhaps, the question shouldn't be
"are we saving time?" rather
"what are we doing with the
time we think we are saving?"

# Kevin Holmes

## The 8088

That old tragic magic
has me
stuck inside Intel
a chip for all seasons

Oh the old 8088
blistering
connected to a 30 meg hard drive 40 pin alive
the size of a
hero sandwich
the 5 ¼ spinning oh the spinning to locate
16 full colors in the EGA
not CGA
two 5 1/4s for copying the flexi
by the score for budding entrepreneurs

and wheels and wheels to
cover security
and ingenuity
to defeat
with color copying
brass tacks
and pie like windows

and the 13 inch
monitors
that failed most often
before the hard drive crashed into itself
carving forever lost into the disk
just short of spinning into infinity

Now
Wow
more power than the old Pentagon
in a chip as big as an old
transistor radio
churning the heat of brains
flipping numbers like sand in the oceans
and
still
a hard drive
2 terror bytes or 49 quadrillion pages times 2 gogaplexes
and Pi leaps to infinity close
and we complain how slow it goes
as it runs our world

# Terry Hume

## Picking Blackberries
### *for Grandma Hume*

We left with the earth damp,
when a long, sheathed finger of mist
hovered above the grass.

Our tin pails swung as we
stumbled over loose rocks and through
a bob-wired fence
bleeding rust.

We huddled together at first
then separated,
fanning and forging,
gobbling the plumpest
for our stomachs.

Our ankles itched as the chiggers bit.
Red welts trailed up to our small knees.
We fought burrs and grappled with thorns
but we always kept our eyes on the prize.

Licked by the sun we made our way home,
like soldiers we trudged after battle.
Our mouths blooming purple,

our hands ink-blotted bruises.

But despite all wounds,
a swift bath cured.
Pajama's clung to our wet haste
as we rushed to the kitchen where
big spoonfuls of flour dropped and
splattered the table.

Making a well in the middle,
Grandma added butter, salt, water
kneading it together until smooth and shiny.
Rolling it out to all four corners and
into a deep baking dish.

A wooden spoon plunged into the rinsed,
sugared berries again and again until
brimming the rim.

Lidded with a second dough
she stabbed the center and
it bled purple then
she dusted the top with sugar.

Four wooden chairs set
in front of the oven,
the light inside beckoned us to watch,
as the cobbler coughed purple bubbles,
the pastry shimmering with sweet.

Our faded purple hands,
rested in our laps,
waiting.

# R. J. Huneke

## Streams

I am addicted to knowledge
Harmfully so
Streams of news, click bait, science, and causes
Despite it all no one comes together
Or at least too few do
Lines are drawn
People's obsession with celebrity
With publicly spewing their own prejudices
Because they
Are
A
Star
Of their own delusional lives
I suffer from this at times too
I am a hypocrite
I am worse . . . actually
I see and I observe
As Holmes would say
Yet I'm hooked on the streams
I can turn it off at any time
But the goddamn Tokyo Ghost is there . . .
Waiting
For the addicts' inevitable
Crawl to the streams.

# Athena Iliou

## I Am Wise

The emotions on waves
Floating away
Detaching ourselves from
Negative words
We rise above

Knowing that we are stronger
Worries about the future
Learning to express the feelings
We act out impromptu scenes
Of growth…routines
Babies to adults
The other growth through communication
Wisdom that connects to it

I am wise

# Maria Iliou

## Hearts of Hearts

Gift of poem
Be observing
Be still
A beautiful thing
Connecting our energies

Expressing my feelings for you
In words...words of silence
Pocketing my emotions
Within my secret heart

You are love of my life
I am passionately deep in
Love with you

Hearts of hearts

Connecting soul of souls
Unwrapping my inner self
Beyond my wisdom

My husband is
Immensely romantic
In his mind...planning

Smiles of joy emerges
Surprisingly bringing home
gifts...for me occasionally
He simply applying
I love you
He appreciates me

Sorrows of lost for words
Words floats in water
Overpowering emotions...I get silly

I'll learn be... mindfulness

Recollection of my memories
Grasping hand in hand in
Marriage...Husband and wife
Listening ear focusing on intensely within
His own words...reciting vows to me
Beautiful moment
Touches my heart of soul
Lovely wedding

Storyteller of narrator
Evocation memories within
Our first sight...immediate attraction
Feelings of deep connection
Beyond our friendship

He embraced me in hug

Declaimer of promises he made
Holds key to my heart
I'm extremely blessed with
Amazing husband

I am your wife then mother
Our first son…born
Amazing experiences
Sharing with you
Journey of years
We were blessed
With our second son
Bundle of joy

My new roles of life lessons

I am photographer,
I am classroom mom
I participate social and
Community activities with our boys
My energies…connects

I am in mommy mode
Scrapbooking of photographs
Storyteller within our boys' gifts
Wisdom of life…joy

# Nurit Israeli

## Blintzes

Mom poured her love
into each and every
one of the blintzes
she made for us.
Hers remain my favorites.

Though she is long gone,
I vividly remember how
she used to pour her
smooth batter into the pan,
tilt it this way and that,

lift, flip, and slide out perfect,
paper-thin, golden crepes,
offering me the first
of the batch, covered with
her homemade strawberry jam.

She would then heap
each crepe with tablespoons
of her indelible cheese filling
that would flood my taste buds
with perfect sweetness.

Mom loved to feed us.
She cooked from the heart,
and when I was old enough
to understand, I greedily
devoured every. single. bite.

I have eaten many a blintz since,
but I still crave the special taste
of mom's savory cheese blintzes,
made according to a special recipe
where the secret ingredient was love.

Evie Ivy

**Another Moon**

On the way home from a dance class, the night
was mild. I looked upward toward the sky.
The moon hung between two buildings across
the street. It seemed large. Don't they say the moon
is drifting away? You would not think it true.
It soon seemed like a yellow and orange
ball behind black branches. A Halloween
moon it could've been. A few feet away
I stopped to breathe deeply, and contemplate
its seeming proximity. It seemed more

a serving of lemon-orange sorbet
on fine navy porcelain, and so pleasing.

# Larry Jaffe

## The Kiss

For my loving wife, because
The kiss was for the next generation
The kiss is for today
The kiss was for yesterday
The kiss is for tomorrow
The kiss is for eternity
The kiss reaches down
The kiss reaches up
The kiss reaches beyond
This kiss is forever

# Kevin Johnson

## People in my dreams

Trying to get the Parmesan cheese off my shoes
And who was that strange executive?
We searched together for a deli
With no success
My how this neighborhood has changed!
What was once rat-infested run-down stores
Is now upscale corporate towers
But no place to get a buttered roll and tea
Now that the only technology I knew
Was chucked by my corporation
Will the strange executive
Find me a new role
Or even a bread roll?

An old friend transfigured
Now with matinee idol looks
Hands me an ice cream cone
Out in the street
Where I am led to meet him
Because I felt he was there
He had a chocolate orange
Long ago when he was sick
Now he is beyond health
He is glorified

Among the lawns
Coming from his house
Coming from my memory
Coming into an early morning dream

I told my buddy over lunch
A farewell before he moved
To the Soviet Socialist Republic of San Francisco
That if the Trade Center ever fell over
It would be lying in the street
In front of the restaurant
Little did I know as I ran around the office
With a box of Swiss muesli
That it was made to collapse straight down
Stuffing t-shirts under the doors
And watching the unimaginable spectacle on TV
Now he has had his jaw removed
And probably exists only in my memory
Hopefully in my dreams
I miss him so

# Gabriel Jones

## Soulmate

See the world from a place beyond the known
Light years travel along a celestial plain

Burn ultraviolet with strays of aqua blue
I see you...

The universe has so much more meaning now
Far apart your mind connects with mine
I feel when your heart smiles

My walks along the edge of the world
I see moments that last a lifetime

In your eyes I use the hue to wash away my strain
Satisfied I am happy to know you

Weightless
suspended in zero gravity
floating, the feeling is unexplained

Strange before we met I had never heard your name
but knew it was you all these years

I get a chance to do it again this lifetime

Soulmate
you can be by my waist-side and I will never let you go
Brush the tears away from face when your spirit feels the woe

The snow never falls when we are apart,
with no moment of heated passion,
we keep the fridge'd hearts

Release the moments when we soon embrace,
and exhale the north winds and soon see flakes

A Kiss from the sun to the moon
Can't escape this fate
my soul belongs us two

# Ryan Jones

## Dawn Of The Second Day

Here is the light, but where is the essence
It was present yesterday, but then died
Before day's end it left
Drained away by the truth
I dared not face it in yesterday's light
Nor in the empty chill that night swept in

It held the clouds, sun, stars, and moon aloft
It kept the ground firm beneath all that walk
It made colors brilliant
It broke labor with joy
It wore spring's flowers and breathed summer's scent
But all this reality took away

Why is the truth initially hidden
Then revealed just to bring about the end
Concealed like snakes in grass
Or cats in undergrowth
Waiting in ambush for the unwitting
In both trickery and in mockery

A different sun rises this morning
Hardly the same thing that rose yesterday
Something is missing here

Something recently gone
The essence that cruel yesterday slew
That source of being that has passed away

# Evelyn Kandel

## Questions

And what of silence
that sooths and comforts
And what of silence
that tears the throat with loneliness
How things change all at once
How things change slowly
Creeping into the mind

And what of trees so lush
laden branches bend and reach
across the road as if to touch
waiting mirrored trees

And when does friendly reaching
become a frightening surge
waving branches dangerous
ready to snatch a tiny car
speeding across the road

And what has this to do with silence
Can questions have answers
when silent moments
drop the cloak of comfort to wear
the long shroud of loneliness

# Barbara Kaufmann

## Day Moon

The reeds make music
In their own greening voices,
They touch one another, like lovers caressing,
And the rustling rises like an anthem.
Sea oats don't ask for second chances,
They just quiver with life,
And when the breeze passes by
They stand in ecstasy.
A falcon rides an updraft,
Above a sun-beaten shore
Not questioning but soaring,
Wings swooshing as it dives to find
An unsuspecting field mouse,
Whose time has run out,
The final screech unheard... except by the wind.
I walk for miles and miles,
My mind wandering and pondering
The evidence all around,
My eyes sting with the yellow of goldenrod,
Born of sand and salt,
My ears ring with the humming of bees
Sucking the last bit of summer.
Late afternoon shadows pull me back
From thoughts that wandered farther than I

Along the beach,
I gather myself up… reluctantly,
Leaving the restless ocean behind.
The wind drums in my ears…
This is your one and only chance…
I sense my breath keeping time with the wind,
Shivering and, at last, seeing it,
I melt into the day moon.

# Daniel Kerr

## The Empty Tomb

Although I have a zest for life,
I am drawn to graveyards,
especially those where famous people rest.
My walks among the dead include visits to
Père Lachaise in Paris,
Recoleta in Buenos Aires,
Trinity Church Graveyard in Manhattan,
Arlington in Washington,
Martin Luther King's Tomb in Atlanta,
The Church of the Holy Sepulchre in Jerusalem,
and *Cementerio de Cristóbal Colón* in Havana.
Often times the tombs speak to us,
words and symbols that tell us how the dead lived, and died,
and often send a message they wanted to us receive after
their death.
Oscar Wilde's tomb says *"he died fortified by the sacraments of
the church."*
At Recoleta, Eva Peron has finally completed her after-death trek,
buried under 20 feet of concrete this time,
safe from future display, adoration, and political manipulation.
Trinity Graveyard teaches us Alexander Hamilton was a
statesman of Consummate wisdom,
*"whose talents and virtues will be admired,*
*long after the marble of his monument has moldered into dust."*

The Eternal Flame burns above JFK's grave at Arlington,
and challenges us to *"ask not what your country can do for you,*
*ask what you can do for your country."*
Water flows at Martin Luther King's grave in Atlanta;
the words of the Prophet Amos are carved in stone,
*"Let justice run down like water,*
*and righteousness like a mighty stream."*

Christ's tomb in Jerusalem is empty,
living testament to the good news of his resurrection,
and ours to follow.
Like most everything else in Cuba,
*Cementerio de Cristóbal Colón* is frozen in time, old, and
decrepit.
The tomb that most caught my eye as I walked among the dead,
was a large mausoleum.
All the doors were open,
And all of the graves were empty.
No one ever rested here,
there are no stories to tell,
at least not yet.
Perhaps sometime in the future,
when I visit the tomb of the frozen in time, old, decrepit,
bearded, dictator,
and his younger brother Raul,
freedom will fall down like rain in Cuba too.
And the people will stop fleeing this island prison,
return to their island country home to live,
and perhaps be buried,
in this empty tomb in Havana.

# Denise Kolanovic

## Your Majesty

Humbly, I bow to you, higher than a skyscraper.
For you are above me in all possible ways.
How so?  Listen here; you are silk and I, paper.
You are intelligence while I'm a dumb stump.
You shine and radiate the Midas touch in rays
Of unearthly power, while I sit on the ledge, bump
Along life counting street cracks and feline strays.
You would never eat leftovers or sing my ditties.
You would never reach into your pocket for a tip.
You would never forecast your morning's drudgery
Nor cascade your worries into your daily itineraries.
You would rather die of thirst than ask for a sip
Of my drink or stop for milk at the pharmacy.
Humbly, I stretch out my hand to yours, a vapor
Of Chanel 95 permeates...a scent you've worn for days
On end.  Now, you fumble in your tapered
Skirt, the slit just high enough to hide a flabby rump,
And tight enough to conceal decades of blemishes.

# Carissa Kopf

## Getting Up In Years

The print on the paper is getting smaller
My memory is getting better at forgetting
Gray weaves through my hair
Is there something wrong with my voice you ask
Nothing at all it's just a song of a wheeze
Don't worry you'll have it one day, too
Funny thing I can't remember what I am writing about
I'm falling asleep at half past nine
Goodbye late shows
My rocking chair feels like a roller coaster
Slow dancing kills my feet
Bowling breaks my back, the ball is so heavy
Fast food and I had to break up
Now what do I look forward to
Mahjong, bingo at five, and afternoon tea
My friends show up in cardigans when it's eighty-two outside
We share a shot of prune juice to regulate our day
And speak of younger years of twenty-five
I stand to stretch
And find a new ache
Off to the doctor's, I set out
I can't seem to find that sore spot
Could it be my elbows, knees, or my heel spur?
The doctor pokes, prods, listens, looks at my mole

Takes my blood and my urine
Half an hour later
He's still not back
A nap is something I'd think about
No worries the nurses said, entering the room
You are healthy as an ox
Is an ox so healthy? I ask myself
Maybe I have no worries
Is it all part of getting old?
Every morning I tell myself it'll be alright
As long as I remember where I left my reading glasses

# Mindy Kronenberg

## Evidence

After the last of the mirrors
were taken down she noticed
the ghost-like, ashen "frames"
remaining on the walls. She painfully
moved to where each had hung
for years, capturing the fleeting
visage of youth and vitality
before the accident. She stood
for a while in front of each faint
rectangle and oval, cameos
emptied of protected profiles,
their outlines
burned into the paint, each
forever a closed portal
to the evidence of her
carefully tended beauty.

# Joan Kuchner

## Play Ball

A car width separating the houses was our stadium.
A strip of grass between the pavements was our ball field.
A girl waiting for the right pitch
learned the language of the game,
how to throw hard and over-handed like a boy.
Then, win or lose,
walked hand-in-hand with her father out of the settling dusk.

# Kate Laible

## And Then The Sun

May the rain fall now, and wash the world around you,
May the sun come out to play another day;
May love come forth, and hold you oh so closely,
The road gets tough; may you find strength to forge a way.

May your good light shine, chase away the looming darkness,
May good light shine, surrounding you in tender care,
May worlds of pain find some peace and even solace,
May the rain fall now, and then the sun shine, by and by.

May love warm you now, then the sun come, by and by.

# Tara Lamberti

## Running Down a Dream

My feet beat on the pavement; one foot after the other I run
towards the house where my father and mother still live. The dips
and bends are the same but the houses look different - and my
friends aren't home anymore. Nobody can come out to play today,
I'm making this run on my own.
I won't meet Joan "half way" down the block, and Rachel's mom
won't yell out the door to come to dinner. I'm running with the
ghosts of Mastic children, myself included. I think about all the
things that were ahead of me and run towards what I can still
achieve.
Strangers mow their lawns and I remember a time when their
home didn't even exist –
it was my playground, a space I vividly remember crawling
through on hands and knees,
listening to the leaves crunch beneath me as I pretended to be
Atreyu crawling through the mud,
and climbing up the tree to speak to Morla, the Ancient One.
Now I feel like the ancient one.
I often think of what it must feel like to be my parents. If I feel
this nostalgia after just 30-some years, what must it be like in your
60s? I picture my parents' memories are in black and white like
the photographs of their youth. And though it might be morbid, I
recently find myself plagued by the realization that they won't be
here forever. I notice I want to spend more time with them,

collecting their stories and adding them to my own.

I want to ensure that I end up settled and successful so they can see me flourish.

I think of all of this when I run.

Sometimes I run from myself, others I'm down a dark spiral into my psyche.

The famous bass of "Stand By Me" plays in my ears, my feet growing heavier with each note. I look down the road, past my childhood home, and out at the Forge River's familiar flow. The horizon ebbs further and further away.

Am I running in place? It's as if the street has become the hallway from Poltergeist and it keeps zooming out of my reach.

And I realized,

it's because I can't run backwards.

# Billy Lamont

## life as a poet: hooked on phonics anonymous

i feel like a jerk
my personality has a quirk
& i hate to network

but you– you are a living action verb
your syntax is superb
can i please have a cover blurb?
***** ***** ***** ***** ***** *****

i'm sorry i tried
wish i could make you a bride
it's just that i am more committed to
living vicariously through poets who have died

i cling to you because i'm in a deep depression
you are a beautiful obsession
but i– i am not your possession!
***** ***** ***** ***** ***** *****

i can't pay my bills
lost all my social skills
but i have a new poem that kills

my boss won't give me a raise

but i can really turn a phrase
please give me your praise!
***** ***** ***** ***** ***** *****

i am easily pissed
an extraordinarily temperamental artist
do you want to be on my guest list?

i live with too much conviction
have to work on my diction
& my bio is fiction
in short, i'm addicted to addiction!
***** ***** ***** ***** ***** *****

poetry & suffering
were sometimes synonymous
until i joined "hooked on phonics anonymous"

# Ellen Lawrence

## fifties favorites

we left it to Beaver
and father knew best
growing up in the fifties
happy days were our quest

everybody loved Lucy
with hair of bright red
and her landlady Ethel
whose husband was Fred

mothers were housewives
wearing aprons and pearls
face always made up
hair in faultless curls

fathers would come home
dressed in suits and ties
disciplined their children
when they told white lies

accepted by friends
with a great family
TV families mirrored
what we all sought to be

the many classics
of fifties TV
they still remind us
how things used to be

Tonia Leon

**Death In The City**

day after day I pass a dead pigeon
near the Rite-Aid pharmacy
on 45 street
could this small corpse
be nestling into the earth?
into the scant earth surrounding the trunk
of a struggling sycamore tree
the only soil
to be encountered
on these paved streets
of Sunnyside Queens

neither I nor anyone else
have gathered it up
to bury him or her in the earth
not even put what
remains of that frozen body
into a plastic bag
and toss it into
the corner trashcan

here the cycle of life is at a stand still
the bird's body
might have nourished other creatures

but no vultures or other carrion consumers
are frequent visitors here
his bones could have
enriched the earth
his feathers - who knows
perhaps flown upward
in illusory prayers

but no heaven is visible from here
god is not denied
but irrelevant passé
a decaying body
carries no meaning . . .

at times I wonder
could the presence of
that dead pigeon
be a test
we're being put to
and all failing?

# Dan Lisle

## Living Lysdexic

Possessed by a backwards soul
Singing in tune
The sun becomes the moon.
Theory of numeric riddles,
Left untold,
Slipping sideways, like flashes of snow.
A source of aggravation,
Sometimes causes elation,
Because I switched my mind.

# Sarah Losner

To see me in the painting
Look beyond the canvas
Where creation was born
And the pink background,
Fitted for a princess.
Look around the people
That fill the picture
With smiles and joy,
Cries and tears,
Comfort and condolences.
Look over the jagged lines
And through the ones
That seem fitted in place.
Look away from the colors,
The angry reds,
The simple greens,
And the woeful blues.
Look not at the places,
Both far and near,
For you won't find me there
Or anywhere.
To see me in the painting
Take a look at the big picture
And you will find me.

–*Can you see me in the painting?*

# Michael McCarthy

## From Somewhere Beyond

Suddenly
walking down a familiar road
yet unaware
of the busted street lamp
above.

Passing a red maple tree
oblivious
to its longevity
and tattered trunk.

I move on
in the haze
of a broken promise.

Nevertheless,
a slow
rather chilling wind
wraps
around my bare skin
evoking a titillating sense
of true love.

# Mollie McMullan

## Scrawny Pigeons

He fed us like we were pigeons,
Time Square our stomping grounds.
We were scrawny,
our wings void of feathers.
He greeted us with bakery bread,
picked out carefully enough to entrap our taste buds.
He was the man with the gifting hands,
the one who made sure to feed us breadcrumbs when we could see
our fragile bones.
However, soon we gained weight,
now too heavy for our jeweled wings to carry us above his head
and into our nests.
The only way to depart from the charming man was to refuse his
crumbs,
shedding our royalties for a chance at freedom.
Sure, we could see our bones,
but once we flew into the grasslands,
we'd be nurtured by the unrelenting compassion of the wild.

# John F. McMullen

## Praying To God

In a Facebook conversation
the other day, an old friend
asked me
*What God do you pray to?*

The question seemed to
make no sense in the
context of the conversation
(*and it turned out that it didn't;
it should have been addressed
to another who mentioned prayer*)

BUT

When thinking about it
is a good question for me
and anyone who prays occasionally
and thinks of a "God"

My Prayer --
-- not the Platters' song
tends to happen only
in church and I tend not to

ask for any gifts or global changes
I think that that stuff is
already done – or not done.

However,
It is still a good question
and leads to even a better question
*Who or what is this God*
*(if there is such a being)?*

After all, Christians
(of I am one)
Jews, Muslims, Hindus,
and so many others
all have their own
concept of a God and
were even willing to
kill others who
held different concepts
(while calling their
own religion peaceful)

Can we not find a common
definition that allows us to
both understand "God"
and live in peace?

# Gene McParland

## Cigarette Moments

Is this the moment?
Nope...still have work to do.
The day is moving on;
lots of moments out there still,
but it's not the right moment yet.
Still working on my project,
and then I will need to clean-up.
Well, I might cut some corners
there though.

Moment by moment by moment
then Bingo!
The right moment is here.
That kickback your heels, sit down
and have a cigarette moment.

Shit!
 I just realized I don't smoke.

A perfect ciggie moment,
and I let a healthy lifestyle
screw it all up.

Maybe I should start smoking?

# Joe Maldonado

## Second opinion

I don't know why I read the review
but I did
and was overcome with the seven stages of poetic grief
neurons tingled
sweat began to bead
I wanted to take a sledgehammer
to my MacBook keys
felt I should set my books ablaze on the wood heap,
watch my words become embers
swept away with the breeze,
thought maybe I could wander off
to a tiny cabin on a mountainside
hide my poems under a floorboard
so they'd never be seen,
or jump into a DeLorean
with a scientist, wild eyed,
fly back to 1999 and smack the pen
from the hand of a younger me

Yet nowadays
I realize
though five stars may be sweet
the feel of a smile starting to creep
as that last syllable leaves
is all the opinion I need

# Lynda Malerba

## The Neighborhood is Dying

The neighborhood is dying!
One by one
Falling away
Leaving gaps
Shattering little hearts

The lure too powerful to logically consider the consequences
Lost to the epidemic
Never to have breath again
Lives shortened by decades

Tears cascading over open caskets
Lessons learned the hardest way
Inconceivable permanence

Farewell to all, their love remains but they have exited their vessel

# Maria Manobianco

## Alabaster Stone

*Sculpture by Maria Manobianco*

asleep in timeless potential
suspended in solid space
I dare to release you
break you from bondage
secure your freedom

but I must know you
before invading your skin—
feel with hands and heart
embrace ragged hills
and valleys of your surface

empty myself of myself
make room for your message
reach your truth
pray you allow my intrusion
to guide my hand

blind with trust I hammer
with widest chisel blade
work all directions
chipping hard and fast
until resistance lessens

exchange chisel
for ones with narrow blades
work slower, more diligent
aware I am closer to your release
I put away my blades
sand paper, fine to finest

white alabaster dust
covers your surface like a veil–
I place you under cool water
reveal closed eyes
a scarred cheek
   and I know your name
     *Buddhic Warrior*

# Cristian Martinez

## Just Be Yourself

Why would you want to be someone else?
When you could be better,
By being yourself
Why pretend to be someone you are not?
When you have something they haven't got
Cheating yourself of the life you have to live
Deprives others of that only which you can give
You have so much more to offer by being just you
Than walking around in someone else's shoes
Trying to live the life of another is a mistake
It is a masquerade, nothing more than a fake
Be yourself and let your qualities shine through
Others will love you more for being just you
Remember that God loves you just as you are
To him you are already a bright shining star
Family and friends will love you more too
If you spend the time just being you!

# Julia Menges

## Fake Myths

Do not tell me that my myths are fake

Tell me of Achilles
the hero who means
"sorrow among these
People."
He, who was not burly
or muscled
but could throw warriors
with his bloody knuckles.

Tell me of the shock he earned
and the life he lost
through his only weakness.

Tell me of Icarus;
the excited boy,
the happy sun,
who in his great escape
flew too close to one.
Tell me of how his wings melted,
how they scorched his skin
as he fell,
and tell me how he was eaten

by the currents,
how he still smiled
in the swell.


Tell me of Orion,
the hunter,
and how he fell in love
with Zeus's daughter.
Tell me how as soon
as she knew
an arrow of
her own flew—
struck him down
and made him blue.


Tell me of Medusa
but not of the monster.
Tell me of the victim,
the priestess,
and of her slaughter.
Tell me we do not still
live in a world, where
for men's sins
women are killed.


Tell me of Persephone,
the curious girl that
ate a seed to set her free.
Tell me how
she embraced her darkness—

tell me of the iron queen
and just because of how she looked
that her power remained
unseen.

Last, tell me of Psyche
of "spirit" of "soul"
that for her lover
she was so bold
to look upon his face
in the hollowness of night
to find that he was a god, and
the heartbreak left from his flight.

Do not tell me my myths are fake,
I will assure you
that the stories
left in wake
were more real
than you ever knew.

# Susan Meyer

## Memories of Spain

Sun drenched Marbella in southern Spain, where beaches
spread out
like afternoon tapas in Torremollinos, reveals piquant scenarios.
Here, you'll gulp grateful sips of salt air, under an almost
full moon,
sporting dreams of languid bedfellows, ravishing Dulcineas and
Lotharios.
We honor rich Iberian culture, entertain splendor in Pablo Picasso,
Don Juan de la Cruz, Don Quijote de la Mancha from Miguel
Cervantes pen.

Wild on the way to see famed Moorish architecture, The
Alhambra, in a compact rental car we dubbed 'the roller skate,'
Late and determined, we raced the Spanish 'policia' with success.
Reflecting now, how the pilgrimage becomes the destination;
our take at the end of the day… shows as dreamy fishing boats
hunt by the sea, drawing up fresh sardines and mollusks served
later with a potato omelet tortilla that speaks tradition here,
like the crusty 'pan' bread, shades of olives, Manchego cheese.

Spain's offerings enliven hearts with salt and sun's glistening
Treasures pledging us remember, when the moon comes up
how amber hand-thrown glasses with Malaga wine and sherry
enhance a pilgrim's Faith with visions… like gypsies dancing
amid hand & guitar strokes of Flamenco, Tarantella, tambourine.

# Edmund Miller

## Sunstroke

Other daffodils
Wrestle for light while one
Stands straight, bathed in sun.

Illuminating
The low-lying clouds,
The sun glows—then sinks.

Dusk clouds mask the orb
But irregular sunbeams
Backlight powder blue.

Now the sun sets flames
To char undersides of clouds
Since black night is near.

Halos of sunlight
Intersect puffs of gray cloud
To highlight the blues.

In every raindrop
Throughout the solar eclipse
A crescent sun shines.

The black disk of moon
Clips the orange disk of sun
And usurps the day.

# Lisa Mintz

## Comfort Zone

I'm not ready to leave, yet I don't want to stay,
and I'm tired of giving my power away.
With a song in my heart, and a new found zeal,
and the knowledge that only love is real…

It's time to reset, to start at square one
and see where it takes me, because this is not fun.
So, I'll leave for a while, and when I return
If nothing has changed, then, this much I'll have learned:

If you want to expand, if you're ready to grow
You must step into the new and just let your life flow,
You can't start a new course while holding on to the old,
Take a leap of faith, it's time to be bold.

I'm ready to grow, I'm about to expand,
because staying in the past & keeping my head in the sand
will not take me to where I want to go,
So, I'll keep moving forward,
and just let my life flow…

# Rita Monte

## Dear Moon

Dear moon
do not be afraid
tonight
do not hide
behind the clouds
I know
it's scary
up there all alone
but know that you are not alone
for the universe
needs you
seeks you
wants you…
Come out
to light the darkest nights
come dear moon
give us your glow
your light

tonight
tomorrow
for eternity

# Jo Mooney

## Good Morning World......

Balmy and still, no night breezes to stir the air or rustle the needles of the tall pines that surround me.......It approaches 5 a.m. and soon the songbirds will fill the air with their chirps and whistles and the music of a new day........Squirrels will dance through the undergrowth and scurry up trees in search of building materials for a new nest......The songbirds gather as well, collecting string, paper, assorted remnants in their backyard playground, their instincts guide them....The sky is dark still and stars twinkle through the pines, providing a serene and beautiful backdrop....a stage on which to present nature and all its wonders........

# Peter Morrison

## My Broadway Baby

I met her standing behind the back row of the theater,
about to watch Cabaret,
Standing for six dollars.

She said her name was Sally; I said "John."
She was there to watch the star,
The one playing Sally Bowles.

She wanted to know how it was done, the performance,
She would audition for the road company.
She invited me to an après-show at the Algonquin.

I walked, she skipped and sang, "Life is a Cabaret..."
In a frivolous soprano voice--
Not well.

At the hotel bar she invited me to her room,
I declined, left, wishing her luck.
In the street I muttered, "She won't make it."

Has anyone ever heard of Sally Something-or-Other?

# Joseph Munisteri

## Pekinese peeking up at me

My new dog is an alien
I don't know why,
But I'm just sure he is.
His name, Logan
The dog is obviously a cleaning robot,
But I'll get to that later,
First though,
Grumpy growls as I leave for work
Then he cries for food by day end
What a sly lil one.
For he was dropped into my life
And
He knows it
And he knows that when she is not around
The food is off the table
For I give in to his begging
As I give him my table scraps
We look at each other
Eye to eye
And promise to keep our secret to ourselves
Else she finds out
We both get in trouble
And the scraps he gets will end
So when that happens

Logan will be renamed roomba

His tiny feet with fur dragging against the floor

His drool dripping as he licks his chops

I accidentally intentionally spill some dinner on the floor

So our new roomba

Can clean up the mess

Suck up the food like a vacuum

Then wash it with extra drool

Followed by a final wipe

As he walks over the spot

with his tiny paws and fur dragging against the floor.

Then finally as I look down,

I see,

A Pekinese, peeking back up at me.

# Marsha M. Nelson

## The Locked Door

I snapped a striking image
last summer, on my way
to Diane Frank's writing retreat
in San Francisco Bay.

A rosebush stretched itself
in the radiant summer sun—
the smell of honey and lemon,
a hint of clove, mingled
with the morning breeze—
crept over ornate wrought-iron
to reveal a single yellow rose
hanging gracefully.

She adorned an auburn, cherry oak door
nestled in a unique cacti garden.
It beckoned me closer.
If I'd walked the cobbled pathway there,
placed my fingers on the brass door knob—
What secrets would I have unlocked?

How strange to know that sometimes,
we're locked behind doors of sadness,
fear and hopelessness, yet embellished
with greatness!

# Donna Nolan

## Suicide

They stand around a deep dark ditch
The tears in their eyes come alive
Unfamiliar faces in an unfamiliar time
What's happening here
Why do they cry
Dressed in black with ghost-like faces
They gather around the site
To pay their respects to their dearly departed
Who was defeated in his contest with life

# George H. Northrup

## Road Rage: an Introduction

He'd like to wring their rubber necks,
those drivers slowing down to watch
the EMS at auto wrecks.
He'd like to kick them in the crotch.

He'd like to smash their SUVs
and leave their bodies in the road
as gasoline leaks past their knees
and engines one by one explode.

He'd cut their heads off for display,
impale each one upon a lance,
and post a warning sign to say,
"Do not slow down to steal a glance!"

# Joan Vullo Obergh

## Capture the Light

Like lightning bugs in small glass jars
I captured moonbeams in the night
until my childhood visions
could envision nothing else.
Someone once wrote that
*no one sees stars*
*when the moon is full.*
Truth be told
I have been bewitched
by moon's solemn face
since I was a young child.
High on the third floor,
long windows flooded my room
with fairy light, mystical and mysterious.
Drowsy, even half-asleep,
my spirit drank it in
until tall apartment houses
across the street finally blocked each
silver ribbon of light from my dreams.
All those years, though never aware,
my senses were being flooded
with inner moonlight,
and like a firefly
sharing its precious gift

I now call upon it in each and
every poem I write.
Those who still believe can find moonlight
flashing between
my lines.

# Susan O'bryne

## A Poem for Police Officer Steven McDonald

A Saint is in our midst
In a wheelchair he sits
Forgiving his trespassers
Turning the other cheek
Praying the Rosary
Struggling to speak
A servant of Jesus
A martyr of New York
Seeing only the good
Through days savage and dark
Inspiring sinners
To stop in their tracks
And think of the horror
They can never take back
He brings forth our consciences
As he whispers his wisdom
He will be welcomed with loving arms
Into God's heavenly kingdom

# Tom Oleszczuk

## Grandpa

one spoke no English
had a nice smile
dug ditches to feed his wife
        and five children

the other was taller thinner
quiet, but he ruffled my hair
played a driving game
        brakes-on brakes-off
        repeat
defended me from his harsh wife
he died too soon

now I have the title
bestowed by a two-year-old
he dragged me everywhere on my last visit
we played ball indoors and outdoors
read more, another, another
watched a cartoon
        and another, another

a photo shows us both happy
hugging in the wintry yard
near his kid-sized basketball hoop stand,

under his dad's full-sized one

my second grandson will soon walk with me
talk to me
drag me hither and yon
plead to play ball
to read
to hug

# Rex Patrick

## When Joy Dies

All I ever wanted
was to look into your eyes

Deep blue pools of water
they were my quest, my prize

As lakes are full of life
so too are your two eyes

I see life in you sparkle
as I gaze, I seem to sigh

Alas my eyes are tearful
deep brown with no surprise

Soon shall they turn shallow
as joy within them dies

Thoughts that once brought laughter
now bring only cries

# Marlene Patti

## Today

I am realizing today
I am not where I want to be
because where everyone else
is isn't where I want to be
or what I had hoped for.
I am leaning towards my words,
perhaps my sadness can pay
I can amuse the lonely hearts
I can begin again
as I realize my worth
I am finally here ready to play.

# Mary C. M. Phillips

## Bramble

I shall not dwell upon the thistles
the bramble in which I am entangled
but rather cast my troubles
unto the wind

Allow them, Lord, to scatter
like wild violet across this dry terrain
enable them to transform and glimmer
like flakes of amethyst

across an open forest glade
rich with flora
hope
and new life

# Kelly Powell

## Gilded Bubble Creature

Your often offensive bubbleness
Has lost its effusive bubbliness
And I have been spending
More valuable time
In my own bubble
With other like-minded bubbles
And the loneliness dissipates

Have been going to our old bubble store
A bit robotically
Replacing the evil bubbles
That have popped along the way
That pretended to care
And went on their merry bubble way

Coming out into the light, the heat
From this protective bubble cave
Wind catching
Sounds of popping
Sounds of freedom

# Pearl Ketover Prilik

## In the wind

You told me to look for you in the wind
as we lay on our backs in the cool grass
on that long ago hot summer day
You told me to look for you in the wind
as a breeze lifted and tens of thousands
of leaves rustled in filigree sunshine
floating chestnut blossoms
in our hair – I could not imagine your
leaving any more than I could imagine
the stopping of the wind – solid heat
you were, as my three-year-old self
melted along your side inhaling your turpentine
cologne, your clean hands resting open
on your paint-smeared shirt
My artist, poetic, impassioned paternus
Black hair falling over closed eyes
I inhaled you – into each particle of my being
a canvas on an easel stood off in the full sunlight –
Look for you in the wind and you would be there
I did not know you were going anywhere
did not know that you were comforting an as yet
unborn, yet already fertilized, grief
I looked for you and just as belief was fading
you rose as powdered dust or chestnut blossoms

sprang from your pine splintered box
dancing dust whirling on the wind
I feel the soft whisper of this summer breeze
touch my grown-beginning to-crease-cheek
I feel the fragrance of paint and turpentine
in the wind and in the shimmer
the rustle of flowers drifting
on another hot summer
of filigreed light –
no longer do I
have to look
to see

# Nino Provenzano

## Majestic Tree

What difference
does it make to a tree
who savors its fruits?
The tree does not care! It follows

nature's order, which is
delivering gifts of beauty and
high nourishing purposes.

One wonders: Is it the soil, the sun,
the air, the water? The tree nods in the wind.
But, it is the human
that appreciates, who hungers,

that goes back for more,
gazes at the tree, and with his eyes speaks
without uttering a word:

"Majestic tree, greater than any artist!
You hide the main source of your nourishment.
Your roots skirt stones, rocks,
and filter the wet earth.

Oh! If poets could unlock your secrets

on how to transform mud into branches,
the green of your leaves,

and just like magic unleash
oxygen, colors,
the fragrance of the flowers,
the lusciousness of your fruits.

Majestic tree, divine artist,
poets envy you!"

Stuart Radowitz

## Life in Balance
*Just someone that I used to know*

One day read some of these.
Know who I am.  Know who you are.
The connection is everything.

Taos hot springs, Stavanger Fjord,
a Scotsman named Michael drinking Balvenie.
A young Spanish girl making a U-turn

running me off the road. These
are the peaceful moments before
cancer hits, breasts are cut off, lives change.

The connection is everything.
Spirit matter soars. Synapse of space and time.
The gap between then and now.

The old brick house showed its age.  Crumbling
mortar, cracks near the windows, patched concrete.
Rickety stairs lead inside.

You lived upstairs and sometimes at night
I would see you looking out the window.  The noise
of the trucks and ambulance always

bothered you. One night looking out you said
"Don't be afraid, you can go in me."
Now steam rises

off my coffee. Today
the front of our house is stone.
Cars drive by. Boys play basketball.

But the back is still untamed trees, branches
down, a dirt and sod space
inhabited by my tortoise.

# Megan Ramirez

## Mo Chuisle

Mo Chuisle,
You are
A pulse
In the veins of existence
The reason that
The flow of life
Keeps oscillating

Mo Chuisle,
You are
A smile born
And
Adored
Straight from the realms
Of the sun
A beam of light
A current that giggles
It's way
Through us

Mo Chuisle,
You are
The only purpose for

Love to bloom
In the cracks of
This broken-hearted world
More than tactical
Behind and beyond
The dimensions of practical

Mo Chuisle,
There is no reason
To face the music
When we are
Born to dance to it
The song a gift
The dance
A thank you
For a life
Well lived

Mo Chuisle,
You are
A twinkle in eternity
Born impeccably chiseled
From the epitaph of creation
–
Always loved
–
Always Worthy
–
Mo Chuisle,
Look up

You are a child
Made of pure love
And that
Mo Chuisle
Is more than
Enough

*Mo Chuisle – An Irish Gaelic word used to say My Darling/Sweetheart, but literally means my pulse.*

# Karen Ranieri

## I Am Grieving

Yes, it has been months, years since they died
Yes, I should be grateful they are at peace
Yes, I know they are in a better place
Yes, I know they would not want me to be sad
Yes, I have hobbies
Yes, I keep busy
Yes, I know my family needs all of me
Yes, I wish I was with them
Yes, sometimes I feel like dying
No, I am not going to hurt myself
No, I am not over it, I never will
No, I am not crazy
No, I am not obsessed
No, you do not know how I feel
No, it is not a pity party
No, I am not being selfish

I am in pain
I am grieving
It is who I am now, From now on
Just listen
Share a story or a memory of my loved one
Say their name
I will not be offended or upset

I love thinking of them, even if my eyes do not agree

Pure love is never ending
Death has no power over it

# Christina M. Rau

## Habits

My grandmother took to
sleeping with her glasses on
and so I take mine off
to remember that I'm alive
and I'm young
and I still have
all that she's left behind
every single wish
she held in her heart
and still holds
letting them drop from her palm
only when they're about to
come true.

# Leslie Reed

## What He Missed In Me

Only now can I have that conversation with my father
That blossoms in the absence of his presence.
20 years too late.
For my taste.

*This is what he missed in me–*
My lust for the numinous and all things unexplainable.
Thwarted by his acerbic wit.

*This is what he missed in me–*
My love for quantum physics,
and the interconnectedness of all things.
The mysteries of the world that extend beyond
mathematics and matter.

*This is what he missed in me–*
My brilliance.
Not his way of holding court.
More laying in waiting–
biding time and gaining steam.

*This is what he missed in me–*
The intersection of what lived in both of us.
Our fidelity for genuine discourse.

A deference to others first,
leaving us dazed to our own calling.
An affection for righteousness.

We two inhabit the spaces in-between
Where words have small meaning and our inflections
spark the volumes we live into.

His red-beaded abacus and my wooden prayer bowl
touch in the bookcase.
A reunion awaiting us across
the quiet workings of time and grace.

## Barbara Reiher-Meyers

For we who dare to share
The sisterhood of poetry
With those who showed the way
Through humor, blood or tears

Who faced the fear and ridicule
By telling secrets no one sought to hear,
The fears that no one ought to bear,
Who cried with every stroke of pen,

I offer you my hand
To raise you into sunlight
From the darkness of your fears.

# Phil Reinstein

## Passionately Poetical

You can be
a poet and you know it    come with me
jump jivin' jamboree
sit right down and right yourself a letter
somber funny rhythm runny pretty witty

Scratch a line
just do it if you screw it up it's fine
any nameless shameless rhyme
move that cursor voice a verse of
passion pounding punch
allegories inside stories    ballads by the bunch
fare thee well my villanelle  haiku words too few  adieu
poetry

Dial a style
Timber timing meter mining take a little while
onomatopoeia will see ya smile
compilations connotations hyperbole imagery
sonnets stanzas word bonanzas metaphor and simile
Coltrane's quatrains quite musical to me
A whacky ode or tacky toad   it's poetry BABY

Lauren Reiss

## Mother of the Midnight Mist

My mom was a spirit who would float above pain
in the cloud-mist of midnight, never to be hurt again.
As an orphan she ran from a terror-filled childhood,
straight into marriage, and then into motherhood.
Motherless, fatherless, she wandered her life
in search of her identity, more than "mother" or "wife."
She studied and crafted herself from within,
but terrible loneliness always flowed 'neath her skin.
I, child caught in midnight madness, listening to Mom's fears,
sitting at her feet, drowning in both sets of tears.
Anger and rage swelled up in my breast;
I prayed one day her identity would be confessed.
In the cruelties of life, I have felt myself smothered –
having a mother who, herself, had never been mothered.
She carried her sadness like a yoke on her back.
Over the years we watched her spirit crack.
Her mother and father took their secret to their grave,
of the life they had spawned and the love they never gave.
Mom's skin turned to parchment, her hands ice to the touch.
Still, I ache to tell her I love her so much.

My mom always pointed out beauty to me,
in the ocean, a poem, or a big sprawling tree.
Those are the places where I find her now,
carrying the mist of midnight as her trailing shroud.

# Diana R. Richman

## Living Connection

The placenta is cut as the first cry is heard,
The placebo attempts to reduce imagined pain,
The poem is written when the voice seeks expression,
The poet's essence becomes visible
By providing a connection.

The young child enters school as the tears are observed,
The candy treats are offered to reduce expected fear,
The canvas is painted when the eyes seek expression,
The artist's essence becomes visible
By creating a connection.

The adolescent begins dating as anxiety appears,
The avoidance increases to stop rejection from peers,
The drama is staged when the emotions seek expression,
The actor's essence becomes visible
By re-enacting a connection.

The young adult rebels as independence is sought,
The addictions overwhelm to divert from grown-up thoughts,
The dance is choreographed when the body seeks expression,
The dancer's essence becomes visible
By moving toward a connection.

The mid-life adult struggles as family balance ebbs and flows,
The escape from responsibilities helps return to a withering soul,
The story is written when the spirit seeks expression,
The writer's essence becomes visible
By sharing a connection.

The mature adult feels longing as mortal awareness is
encountered,
The recognition of limitations serves to act on true desires,
The melody is played when the emotions seek expression,
The musician's essence becomes visible
By orchestrating a connection.

The soul leaves its body as the last breath is heard,
The placebo reflects reality of life aligned with chosen words,
The poem is a revelation of the spirit's true expression,
The human essence is now visible
By life lived with authentic connection.

# Al Ripandelli

## Unseasonable

Heated air
forms warm wind currents that
convey the musty scent of roasting leaves
and drying trail beds
once damp from the winter thaw.
Hints of decay
within fragrant wisps
from freshly opened buds and extruded resins
revitalize the dormant spirit
through olfactory gestures
of pine needle tinged
airborne oak tree pollen and mold spores.
Arousing hope as they meander through the centers of memory
and emotion
and provoking sadness
of a future without those lovers stolen from us
by delusion, disinterest or death.

# Rita B. Rose

## Apparition

In my black Victorian rocker with gold leaf trim
Your ghostly voice crackles as chair and you refuse to be stilled
How in the airy faint hallway your scent embeds in a
parapet whim
Heaven knows you are somewhere here of your own robust will

In my dark varnished kitchen I sip a spot of Poe Tea
Flame of the lamplight rises— Chimney, I know it was low!
And content in seat, I entertain a wintry draft; aware you
follow me
Across the Rosewood table you drift; only a stones' throw.

Nighttime offers rest, allowing me to nap in living room
Awakened— I rise— familiar with creaking spirit of you
As fireside tinder warms; rescuing me from hasty gloom
I dare to peek amid webbed fingers; to see your waif-like
form near flue

Nothing— is more for me to do; I find and climb my way upstairs,
Muttering for you to leave
Shouting while on top of landing, "Apparition, I wish to retire,
provide me a peaceful reprieve."

# Marc Rosen

## In The Hero's Kitchen

I sit in the hero's kitchen
Both our laptops open, reading email after email
The same woman who aided the drag king
Who threw Stonewall's first punch
With a right hook of her own
Swapping stories with me as we review poem after poem,
Poet after poet, seeking additions to her legacy
We break for pizza, to stretch, to per her dog
Hour after hour, until we were done, and all I could think
Was that without her, I would leave no legacy for Stonewall

# Narges Rothermel

## An Ode to Walt Whitman

A messenger

Was anxious on that rainy day
I was trying to find my way
held my breath ignored the haze
till I saw Walt Whitman's place.

Felt sorry for not visiting him earlier
didn't have an excuse for my failure
It wasn't the right time for blame
Excitement disguised my shame.

Took a deep breath and entered the hall
Faced picture of Walt Whitman on the wall
I said in silence to beloved poet of the Island,
"I'm a traveler, a wanderer from another land.

I have come from the famous old-Persia
The one that was once, Jewel of the Asia,
Treasures of Rumi, Hafiz, and Saadi are alive in her core
the land of Ferdowsi, Omar Khayyam, and so many more."

As if guided by spirits of poets from the ancient land,
I greeted Walt Whitman, the Great Poet of Fish Island

Bowed my head and delivered greetings as my holy chore
Spirits of Persian Poets by my side, I was anxious no more.

Dear Walt Whitman, Happy 200<sup>th</sup> Birthday

# A. A. Rubin

## The Beating of my Heart

The beating of my heart
The syncopated thrum
Rising from my chest
A cacophony of drums

I lose myself in action
My nervousness is gone
I rise up in the moment
To each challenge as it comes

The outcome's still in doubt
My fortune's not yet spun
Will I be left standing
When the day is done?

Adrenaline runs through me
In my veins it hums
I hope it will sustain me
Through the Sturm und Drang

The battle now is over
And victory is won
Bards of it are singing
Ballads now are strummed

My heart again is racing
Remembering the scrum
That was really scary
But man, it sure was fun

Lady Samantha

**Writer's Block**

I feel like I have writer's block again
Complete stasis, perhaps boredom
Words are crumbling like little bits of feta cheese
Into a chaotic pile of letters
Nothing seems to fit on the page
I try to arrange the letters like Scrabble tiles
Only gibberish ensues
Squall lines pass through words,
Words that are drowning in a cacophony
of grunts and frustration
I try to save them, stet
But, alas! I have to let them go
My page has no room left
I crumble the paper and turn it into a projectile
I throw it from the other side of the room
Into the wastebasket
Three points!

# Robert Savino

## Phantom Pigeons

I remember when an apple a day
was for the teacher
or to keep the doctor away,
when a hand raised to ante up
a question was dealt the truth.

Time has evolved from hand-
carved hieroglyphics to cosmic
conductors of airborne waves
through eyes of immutable doubt
where little separates the truth
from a bowl of alphabet soup.

I've collected enough birthday
candles to feed pigeons in the park,
drift in rhythm with slow falling
feathers and scrutinize my timepiece,
listen to the tick-tock,
occasionally miss a beat . . .

and voices that haunt me.
They know where to find me,
before time goes dark.

# Andrea Schiralli

## Learning to Love

Your first kiss dies in a motorcycle--
Your first--
CRASH
with reality.
Your soulmate gets engaged
to your (ex) best friend
Look at their fancy city lives,
cocaine and cocktails
vapid vanity.
The one who stole your heart (and purity)
comes out of the closet
[*no wonder he couldn't cum.* relief]
You find another "soulmate"
[*i swear, this time he's The One*]
Destiny may not be in the stars
But it's certainly in his eyes
You marry!
    ecstatic
    erratic
    dramatic
Divorce.
This time, your heart doesn't break.
It shatters.
[*love is for fools. i will never love again!*]
But the clock continues to tick ...

   ...

So you settle--for less than magic--
and a part of you dies
But is reborn,
You're transformed
in her star-studded eyes

# Karen Schulte

## Vanished

Even for the bravest of hearts
each of us walks with fear.
The small knot we knit within us echoes
the last drumming.

Beyond what we see and feel
there is a universe so vast
it does not acknowledge mere mortals.
Everything bends to its path.

After a great wind,
my overgrown arborvitae bows to its roots.
The porch light's fluorescent glow
singes and tears an insect's wings.

We forget to remember
to anchor the tree, dim a bulb.
Outside the back door
the timpani of metal upon metal
chimes whenever the breeze moves.

Even though we issue proclamations
pass laws, make judgments
we all know we are sinking into the oceans

and the oceans are floating with plastic and toxic waste.
Animals we name by sight are vanishing,
we can hardly breathe or see the empty sky.

Still the universe, filaments of matter,
galaxies, constellations, are pursued
by an energy, a void whirling and growing,
a force beyond us unknown
except in equations and theories.

Our realm of life and love
is disappearing, no one knows
when lights will fail and go dark.

We are dying…
and the universe knows nothing of us.

# Ron Scott

## Welcome Home

Information Day for Vietnam vets.
The crowd is a little thinner this year
Plenty of parking spaces
*Handicap* stickers unnecessary
Walk right in, if able
Wheelchair accessible, if not

Veterans Hospital at Northport our host
Data exchange a mutual goal
Filing a claim will take its toll
Physical deterioration combat related?
Rule number one, they say
To determine who will pay.

Topics of the day:
Making a Positive Impact on Your Health
Post-Traumatic Stress Disorder
Sorry, Agent Orange didn't make the cut
Aging clouds diagnosis
So much for my psychosis.

Northport is impressive
The golf course is lovely
Rank does have its privileges

Once I had rank
A long time ago
When I could walk.
Today, I converse with strangers
But they are not strangers
We are brothers
We smile and nod
In our collective pain
Welcome home.

# Robert Seck

## Then and Now

The mills have closed
But the water still runs
It don't take much
For the children to whimper
Not that much here
For the old folk to smile

Her bell bottoms have since
Faded they bear old hopes
Distant joys less familiar
Still in the air
Whisked away somewhere
Wherever you may go
You may come back out
Where you are

May it just be

It pains her for that moment
To rejoice in a smoke
Her youth was such a rush
And now
She hides just to feel
Empty eyes carry blank

Faces speak a careless
Whisper

Her love is somewhere else now
Running in fields dancing
In mud
Now she lives memories ought
Not to be forgot
As she lay to rest her
Love upon the cot

# Harriet Slaughter

## Counting the Fridays

Counting the Fridays is like
Counting the yesterdays
Peeling off the weeks
Like layers of skin flaking into thin air.
Counting time.
Why do we do this?
Counting time, always counting time
Into seconds, minutes, hours, days...
What does it mean?
It's Friday again!

# Emily-Sue Sloane

## Leisure Day at the Beach

Tide's in again
Gentle waves push forward
to cover the North Shore's rocky beach
subdivided by seaweed-stained ropes and signs
declaring who can and can't stay,
where swimming is allowed or not
The gentle waves carry out their own rhythm
when they move out
a greened slice of shifting sand
dries in the midday sun

Rotting algae scents the air
something to get used to
like toughening your soles
for walking the narrow stripe that separates
green trees from the blue-black sea

Neither gulls nor cormorants care
about the lines and signs
striating the shoreline into tiny provinces
of haves and have-nots

A crow screeches, struts by,
the last of three I see spaced evenly

across my square of beach—
public space any crow can frequent
Tired of land fare, they feast on sea-spiced delicacies
The gulls give a wide berth to these jet-black gangsters
who stride proudly through the buffet
revealed by the ebbing tide

Almost imperceptibly mackerel clouds move in
to block the blue-filled sky
the sun fades to a hazy blur
the reaching hands of coastline drift outside color now,
muted tones herald the day's shift in character
Boats moored beyond the swim ropes
twist and turn in the breeze,
lazy clanking ropes on masts call out
their desire to drift with the wind's whim

A lone egret stands ankle-deep in the middle tide
white on gray
until in a flash it's gone
Missing morning's clarity, I too abandon the waterfront

# Barbara Southard

## In the Hospital Bed Next to Mine

She, lying oh so still on her back,
swollen belly overtaking her ravaged
body, checking where in relation
to reach, her glass of water will be,
bucket of ice, buzzer,
overhead light pull—yes
—her eyeglasses—
where are her glasses?

Checking again, then again,
like a soldier checking gear
before night maneuvers—dusk
turning to dark—the sound of
a train drifting in the open window—
feet, like the sound of scattering mice
outside the doorway.

I hear her repeat again and again:
*I can do this. Ice  water  nurse*
*oh oh ice  yes  please  ice.*

I wait for her family's return to her bedside.

Let morning come. Let fingers of sun

reach inside the room, her husband
whisper in her ear
*Here, hold my hand.*
Let Morpheus carry her through the day.

# Dd. Spungin

## While considering the mermaid

What would I miss most?
The mermaid cannot walk
Nor can she run

Don't speak to me of love
Or loving
This fish out of water

Tucking her secrets
Into that green gillfold
Paying taxis

Don't speak of love or loving
Split personalities are nothing
Beside her unsplit jail

Would I be beautiful
Desirable
Sing sailors to their ends?

I can do that:
Crazy-glue divisions
Lock love out

237

Swim alone
Walk out of the sea
Run risks.

# Toni-Cara Stellitano

## My Mother

I had an astrologer read my birth chart once, and ask me if I
was an orphan.
Neither one of my parents are deceased,
Let that one sink in.

I built a life around what I did not receive,
softening my shoulders when the wind blew strong
through the lives of others,
Dispersing the softness that was absent from the jagged cliffs of
my childhood,
and watching it pour from my hands like water.

Standing in the shower in the second grade, a river running over
my head, trickling down my arms and gathering in cupped hands.
.

"God's Love," I thought, "Pours endlessly from above,
It is I who will give it away."

An image of the Virgin Mary
.

I don't know what to say about my mother.
I learned about compassion at 17 from an Eating Disorder
Therapist named Kathy Cortese, who used to rub her upper arm
softly each time I would cry, tilt her head and say, "Be so gentle
with yourself."

My pain, My pain, My pain.
Always held from across the room,
Once a week,
by a woman who was not my mother.
By a Woman who is not my Mother,
Still.

.

(This hurts)

.

She is 71, and She is desperate to hold me.
The cliffs of my upbringing have risen like SPOKES from the
SKIN
that she found too raw to touch back in the days when it was soft,
and ready to receive her.

(No, no! I won't meet the NEED in you that I have SCOURED
THIS LIFE AND THIS BODY to MEET in ME! NO! NO!
Anger...This Child)

...But My Mother, My Mother, My Mother...

Standing there in the kitchen,
Thirty-four years old, baby in her arms,
swaying and weeping the pain of her history
into the arms of that child,
Nowhere else to bring herself,
but there to the arms of that child.

.

My Mother. My mother. My Mother.

# Ed Stever

## Lost Vegas

She said, "I'm leaving.
I'm going out to Vegas,
and I don't need any baggage."
So she stepped toward the
open fifth floor window,
locked bird cage in hand,
and released it into
the afternoon sun.
The yellow canary felt
the rush of fresh air
and thought it was free,
because it could fly.

# Lennon Stravato

## The Inner Dialect

I am consumed by duty for which I do not know relief
a certain type of faith, not predicated on belief
fidelity to that voice, with which I must connect
speaking language of the heart – an inner dialect

No longer can I be conscribed by circumstance
to pursue the dollar, and to my dreams look askance
for life is best lived, when heart is the architect
and its plans are penned in the inner dialect

And I struggle with this world, broken by insularity
where greed has risen but love is given with austerity
for each being should find dignity and respect
and law must yield to the letter of the inner dialect

But if when my song to me seems adequate
spirit speaks: "your god in human words is counterfeit"
I'll know each allusion does not to meaning-itself reflect
and I have betrayed the lyric of the inner dialect

Then every last word, by my own hand, I will unweave
for this religion does adorn, so poorly, a human sleeve
and only when I can strengthen anyone who does inspect
might my words have been spoken, with that inner dialect

# Douglas G. Swezey

## #1420 (Honeymoon Phase)

I see our phases in everything
There are phases to relationships
They say the first
Moon of a marriage
Is the sweetest
Therefore named after honey

There are phases to sound waves
A vibration of Thin Air
Sounds are changes in air pressure
A ripple of a stone in water,
Sound is created by movement in air
Waves comprised of peaks and troughs
When the same frequency and phase are used
In Constructive Interference, two waves combine
To create a single sound of greater amplitude

And there are phases of the moon
As it circles the earth
Showing different sides of terrain
Illuminating different paths of thought
Waxing & waning, gibbous & crescent,
New, full, & blue

There are phases to power
Three-phase is a common polyphase method of AC
Generation, transmission, and distribution
One can convert Phase A, B, and C power wires
To single phase by converting to DC
Back to single phase AC
Using a rectifier to convert three phase AC into DC
And an inverter to convert back to single phase

There are phases to each matter
Whereas we once were
A light and airy effluvium
We have liquefied
Our components have swirled
And now are solid

There are phases to color
Varying with development, age or season
Red foxes can be red, black, silver, or crossed
Black bears can be black or brown,
Cinnamon, blond, blue-gray, or white
The tail feathers of the Ruffed Grouse showing
Gray, red, intermediate, brown and split
Screech Owls red or gray
Each phase depending upon a change
In Nature's seasons for breeding or survival
Sometimes I turn red when I see you

The moon has turned to gold
It lights me up like plasma

A solid stentorian sonic boom
When you electrify me
A neon sign of love

There are phases to phases
A phase is a stage or step
One can phase in a stage or point of advancement
Or phase out by stopping operation, practice or production
Or one can be fazed when their behavior changes
Always something transitive

There is nothing transitive about this period
This is no phase – it is a cycle
Each moonrise a new adventure
Each sunrise a chance to repeat again

# Wayne Thoden

## I've Paid The Price

The sun bestows its amber glow,
Birds' sweet songs fill the air.
Coddled dreams return to sleep
Unspoiled from the wear.

Zephyr wind blows flowered fields,
Awakening the senses.
Reflections of a lover past
Squelched by my defenses.

Have I not paid the price for love?
Felt sorrow's sad caress
Beguiled by beauty's sweet disguise,
Enamored and impressed?

But, ask me not to try again.
No, that path I'll not wander
On unknown heartaches still to come,
My feelings not to squander.

# J R Turek

## Room With A View

Double-wide window looking out at 3-story brick building,
tall glass panels reflect bright sky, fluorescents flank ceilings
to the right, parking garage left, a small flock of birds fly
across mirror surface in search of breakfast
but I'm too nauseous to think on that.
Last night, my first overnight stay in a hospital,
the glass reflected stars I'd never seen before, a galaxy in indigo
deepening by the hour, sleepless in a room with a view to healing
after surgery, a universe of possibilities once I am home,
recouping, moving through new days pain-free and with
a freedom to explore anything, to accomplish everything,
to be the view and not the room.

This morning I see a tall tree straddled to the right,
limbs near bare of leaves on this brisk November morn.
Far right I see what looks to be a squirrel nest balanced
in the crooked elbow of limb and branch and wonder
how it remains stoic and straight unlike my forearm plastered
with ports and tape and lines and nurse's kind admonishing to
keep it straight as I hold my new journal filling lines with
amethyst ink to clear my head of low blood pressure concerns
and an ache in my knee at the incision, the construction site
of my new knee promising a stairway of mobility.

Last night, I wondered whether the nest was occupied, a family moved out and settled somewhere new or a new family-to-be perhaps envisioning a new life in a new place but those visions crumbled in daylight.  The nest perched in autumn oak or majestic elm is actually a security light and I just now remember a bright star I wished upon and connect those astrological dots and realize my blazing star wishes were on a light, staunch solid now invisible in bright sun with a pale blue background.
The lower level of clouds scurry in an autumn breeze to steal more leaves from near-naked limbs, and the nurse interrupts time for another pill.

# Janet Wade

## Poetry and Me

There was emptiness in my heart, begging to be refilled
Emotionally drained, demanding more than sympathy could
ever give
Simple thoughts were elusive, begging to be nurtured and caressed
Expressive sighs and wonders needed a threshold to progress

So out birthed "Poetry" to fill that massive gap
Left in my heart by life's uncanny trap
Poetry showed up unannounced and guided me through
The days and nights when I was down and blue

Poetry helped me to laugh at my silly mistakes
Saved me from myself and my growing heartaches
Never criticized, nor point fingers at the weaknesses found
But lifted me up to find an escape to solid ground

In poetry I found a friend who is very loving and kind
One I can share my inner thoughts with and don't mind me on
rewind
I remembered when each love left me, how I wanted to lose
my mind
Poetry took over, with pen and papers my heart it realigned

Now we two are no strangers connected and true

We celebrate each other with poems anew
Listening more intensively when someone else's pen so talk
Applauding each poem birthed knowing Poetry is a
comforting walk

# James P. Wagner (Ishwa)

## The Cone

*"Ice Cream comes in a cup*
*always has, always will!"*
That's what the people thought at the 1904 St. Louis world's fair
on the hot day
when they moved passed
the hot waffles
to get that nice
cool ice cream.
Only 5 cents a cup!
Flying,
flying...
until they couldn't fly anymore!
They ran out of those cups
that the ice cream had always come in
and always would...
Yet gallons and gallons
of the fresh
cool treat remained
with many waiting customers.

A calamity in the making...
until one vendor
looked at a waffle
in a way that no waffle had been looked at before

251

he rolled it up in a cone
and placed a beautiful scoop of ice cream on top.

And with this business merger,
between ice cream and waffle stand
our world change
forever.

# Jillian Wagner

## Let Me Linger Here

Let me linger here
in the warmth of summer
without a chill on my skin.

Let me linger here under the tree
on the hill
on a bed of velvet moss.

Let me linger here,
surrounded by grass spun into gold
by the late afternoon sun.

Let me linger here
overlooking the sea,
salty ocean breeze brushing over my face.

Let me linger here
in this world my imagination
has led me to.

Let me linger here
just a little while longer.

# Margarette Wahl

## Fragile

*"I heard it said, that people*
*come into our lives for a reason...*
*Bringing something to our lives*
*that we must learn and we are lead,*
*to those who help us most to grow*
*if we let them.." For Good, from Wicked*

He is fragile,
most
won't see him
that way.

Hyperactive
twitches in his seat
plays on iPad.
Flapping fingers
crackles his knuckles,
he smiles.

Angry birds temple run
five little monkeys jumping on the bed
baby shark
all *squeak* out his excitement
as he plays or watches.

Deletes apps to arouse
my adult attention.

Sporadic language
random hellos or requests
for food or drink.
He knows only Kosher,
asks anyway,
making sure I do my part
and check.
I learn to read labels hear of Shabbat
learn Hebrew letters and phrases
Find out what it means to be Persian Jewish.
Fragile asks for my tickles
to his ribs for giggles.

Food plates cups paint brushes puzzle pieces
soar across a classroom floor,
hit against the walls
followed by sounds of his laughter.
He's fragile
awaits my reaction,
I simply ask why.

*It is funny.*

*I don't know* his response.

Fragile throws off his sneakers
kicking hitting falling to the floor,
he has difficulty
transitioning through school days,
through life.

He is fragile and I remember
as he runs naked
across the playground,
flushes his clothes
on a visit to the bathroom.

Fragile as he leaps out
for attention,
someone else's child
my response (ability).
I pause and not react.

A triplet at home
or fragile, a face
assigned to share
classroom space with.

Fragile, but when together,

we both learn.

# Herb Wahlsteen

## Karen

She wanted to show off
the gentle beauty of
her white-rose smile,
and the glad gleam of
her green-carnation eyes.

He wanted the gray,
convoluted matter of
her brain out
where others and he
could see it.

She wanted to see him smile.
She wanted to see everyone smile.
She tried to lighten and
warm everyone with
her bright, warm joy.

He wanted only to see
cynical intellectual teeth
cut victims into
small shreds.

Her world was the whole town of

Holbrook, and she worried about
everyone in it.

His world was the cosmos, and
he was overwhelmed with
cosmic despair.

She laughed at him.
He cried for her.
He mocked her.
She cried because of him.

For too long they had
called that "love."

# Virginia Walker

## Inversion

Descending water vapor
obscures the thicket of trees
we contrive the outlines

this transitory clime,
tremulous, prepares us
for peace of isolation

# George Wallace

## In Your Hermitage of Work or Sleep

In your hermitage of work or sleep, where love cannot touch you, and grief cannot touch you, where redemption cannot touch you or trouble or hope, where only the instruments of time, and obligation,

Where i cannot touch you, in your dark hermitage where you relinquish, renounce, abandon, resign, where you start all over again, your cell or cloister, your courtyard of invincibility,

How beautiful! to be left alone! to live religiously and in sweet seclusion, the news of the world stunning everyone else, but not you, safe in your deep devotions and your brethren and mutual exchange of labor,

In your convent of shame and welcome darkness, undisturbed and why do they even bother to try, nothing, nothing, you want nothing, only to work and partake of the bitter pill of duty, forgetfulness and the distraction of sleep,

In your monks-cap and your cloak of prayer,

There i would touch you, where love lies blind, sleeping to the touch, where oblivion is a hovering bird and you ride it like a broom over clay, and you sweep up everything and the songbird singing

The songbird at your window, at your bedside, the songbird in the darkness and in your head

The songbird, which would dispel darkness and wake you to the beauty and the pain of your conscious self, in the light of the world, singing – the songbird, which has stopped singing, which wants to sing again

# Charles Peter Watson

## SOLiloquy

Like a bloom out of wintry ebb,
you breach the bruise hue of morn's sheath,
brightest by being closest by several minutes.
This star that was a god of old,
a light of the lightest elements
is one with the universe.
There are so many millions like you,
so many millions who love you,
who fear you,
who live and die by you.
Alma pater of the celestial trinity
with our Mother Earth as your child
and her barren child around her,
you make the most of the day
for much of the daytime.

# Jill Watson

## Finger to the Button

I put my finger to the button, 3C
Up the 3 flights to the vintage flat
A tarnished brass doorknob
Walls like paper

You kept the door open
Outside, I paused
Smiled
I heard music and you laboring in the kitchen
The spoon hit the stainless steel sink
and it rang like a school bell marking 3:30, the end of the day

I shed my coat and my concerns at the door
Sometimes you greeted me and swept reality under the carpet
I'd ask how you were and you would say, "Better now."
Today, you were topping off a latte
That was our thing

In 810 you taught
Step by step
the intricacies involved
in the perfect foam

Your place, I said, smelled like boy, though you were half way

through your life
The next time
there were fresh flowers and
a candle
But, your scent still erupted in my nose
I excitedly and unconsciously bit my lip and drew in a breath

Matchbox cars loitered the couch,
like you and I on those stolen days
Spread out and open like the books on your table

You castigated Mother Jones and praised the New Yorker
saying you needed to read books more
We were both lovers of words,
the quintessential turn on for us both
I knew it the day I met you
It was your mind that I was afraid of most

And, together, in a room with dust on the fan
and a bed that creaked, we shared moments
Unplanned to both of us
We agreed;
We were never at a loss for conversation

# Amelia Wells

## Where I'm From

I'm from Sayville
I'm from my father's childhood home which is now my
childhood home
I'm from a front yard with tree that has pastel pink blossoms
in the spring
I'm from singing around the house until my throat's dry and sore.
I'm from the safe little town in Long Island with friendly people
wherever you turn.
I'm from "strawberry girl" and "you march to the beat of
your own drum"
I'm from homemade tomato sauce and delicious chicken marsala.
I'm from a light pink room that i've had since I was a baby.
I'm from singing in front a crowd of people, only seeing my
parents faces
I'm from toy "skins" lying around the house and a loveable dog
that wants all the attention
I'm from going out east with my mother and seeing my aunt in
Mattituck
I'm from the town where my family has lived for 6 generations
I'm from going to my singing lessons every friday night

I'm from performing on stage like I've done since I was 2
I'm from boating on the water and going to fire island with
my dad's family
I'm from Long Island, New York
I'm from the past, the present and the future

# Marq Wells

## Dead Man's Shoes
### (Pea Soup part 5)

As he passes over the next rise on HWY 95 on the outskirts of Las
Vegas, whistling some vaguely known tune to himself, Squatter
sings to himself the lyrics of an unknown tune.

"Walking in a dead man's shoes...Walking in a dead man's shoes,
all the dull things spring to life ! Walking in a dead man's shoes !

I've sworn off before with cusses and shouts
but nothing ever really seems the same once
you've found out how it is and just what happens
when you walk mile after mile, passing sign post after signpost
and the miles begin to melt away into some sort
of horrid vision but then I saw that poor soul lying there so still
so rigid and I knew that life had left him.

So I thought (since my own shoes were almost shot)
maybe this Soul's got some good shoes that i could use
and I wanted to shout HALLELUJAH to the heavens

but I remembered that God was probably still pissed
so i figured to try them on anyway and guess what?

THEY FIT!

# Jack Zaffos

## Come Here To The River

Come here to the river,
the river that you know.
The river from high mountains,
rushing down to the meadows,
splashing rocks with a misty spray.

You know the river
you hear the flowing,
it is your path,
it is your life.

Do not fear the jagged rocks,
do not fear the foamy rapids
as you are streamed to places not known.

Please drink this water,
with long deep drinks,
you know the taste,
you know it's cool and clear.

This is the river that holds you with compassion
as you surrender to the flow
towards river banks unseen.

# Thomas Zampino

## Infinite Jaggedness, Finite Wisdom

Beaten back so many times, we steady ourselves for the final
blow, the one that will do us in, the one that will surely
define us. If we only knew then what we know now
(we tell ourselves), we'd have made something
better of our time. Maybe taken that other
road, or gotten drunk one more time. All
a fool's speculation, a buffoon's final
refuge. It's all the same. But we
somehow always knew that,
looking back. Didn't we?

# Donna Zephrine

## Remembrance of 9/11

It is a day no one can forget.

No matter what you were doing the moment you heard the news,
that moment is permanently marked in your memory.

People ran to a TV to find out what was happening.

It seemed unreal, this couldn't be happening, not to our country,
not to us.

But it did.

The news had video of the planes going into the towers.

Even watching it, it didn't seem real.

You might have yelled at the plane through the TV, "stop," "no,"
in disbelief of what you were seeing.

The large fogs of smoke, the destruction, the devastation, and the
men, women, and children running for their lives, jumping from
windows, gasping for air.

As civilians ran out, emergency personnel ran in. Ready to
protect, ready to serve. Some never made it back out.

An attack on America.

The World Trade Center was hit, the Pentagon, and there was a
plan for a hit on the White House.

It is unimaginable how people could plan to hurt so many and
cause such devastation.

New Yorkers felt a special kind of pain, in our town, in our state.

We lost our friends, our family members, our neighbors.

Families searched for lost loved ones for months hoping they

would come home. Praying that they weren't gone forever.
The survivors suffered pain and guilt that is unimaginable.
And from that attack we pursued a war. A war that also cost
a hefty price.
Years may pass but the memories never fade, and those lives are
never forgotten.

# About the Authors

**Lloyd Abrams**, a retired high school teacher and administrator, and an avid recumbent bicycle rider and long-distance walker, has been writing short stories and, later, poetry for his personal joy for over thirty years. Lloyd's stories and poems have been published in a number of anthologies and publications. www.lbavha.com/write

**Donald E. Allen** is a member of the Performance Poets Association, the Bard's Initiative, and The Academy of American Poets. Don has three books of historical poetry: *April 1861*, *April 1862*, and *April 1865*. DonaldEAllen.blogspot.com

**Linda Allocco** is a nature photographer who loves to write poetry, often marrying these two passions together. Linda's work has been published in *Long Island Literary Journal 2017, Poet's Domain Volume 32, Suffolk County Poetry Review 2018, Bards Annual 2018, The Poets' Almanac 2018, Suffolk County Poetry Review 2019, Poets to Come.*

**Sharon Anderson** is published in many international and local anthologies, was nominated for a Pushcart prize, and has four publications of her own poetry with a fifth to be released soon. She serves on the advisory board of the Nassau County Poet Laureate Society, the advisory board for Bards Initiative, and is a PPA host at Oceanside Library.

**Rose Anzick** is the proud mother/grandmother of poets Kate Fox and Rebecca Fox. She has been writing since her mid-20s and has been a regular contributor to *Great South Bay Magazine*. Her second love, and hobby, is photography. She is honored and excited to have her poetry included in this anthology.

**Bob Baker** is a former retail store manager and insurance manager who worked for many years in those fields so he could eat on a regular basis. Now in retirement, his bills might be plentiful, but he has the opportunity to actually write, and write some more, and not just think about writing.

**Claudia Balthazar** is a lifestyle blogger and freelance writer for numerous digital news publications. She graduated from Hofstra University with a bachelor's degree in journalism and Political Science. Check out her portfolio at cqbalthazar.com. Poetry is her first love and forever passion.

**William Balzac** is the author of two books of poetry, *The Wind Shall Hear My Words* (2008) and *The Stars Will Speak Them* (2009). He resides in Deer Park, Suffolk County, New York.

**Christine A. Barbour** is a life-long resident of Woodhaven, NY, and a direct descended of Adam Mott, a founding family of Hempstead, LI. She received a BA from The City University of New York at Queens College, and an MFA in Writing from Sarah Lawrence College, under thesis advisor Vijay Seshadri, 2014 Pulitzer Prize Winner in Poetry.

**Marilyn Barker** started writing an occasional poem many years ago. It is just recently that she's become more interested in improving her skill. She is also an acrylic artist and it is sometimes a challenge finding time to concentrate on both. She sometimes thinks of a book with her artwork and poetry....one of these days.

**Antonio Bellia (Madly Loved)** is a renaissance man who has traveled many paths, a man of deep sentiment drawn to performing arts, who has acted and danced throughout his lifetime, and always compelled to express his emotions and experiences in the form of poetry. He is translating his poems from Italian into English.

**Cristina Bernich**, a local pediatric specialist, is former graduate of Columbia University Teacher's College, NY. Her three busy boys, her work with infants and children and their families, and her love of nature happily fill her days.

**Thérèse M. Craine Bertsch** is a Doctor of Social Work and a published author. Her essay was included in "Visions and Vocations 2018" by Catholic Women Speak, was published by Paulist Press, and her poems were published in the recent *Suffolk County Poetry Review.* She is the mother of 5 children and grandmother to 8 grandchildren.

**Maggie Bloomfield** is an award-winning poet, essayist, Emmy-winning lyricist for Sesame Street, and graduate/MFA Program at SBSH. Her chapbook, *Trains of Thought,* was published by Local Gems Press, and *Sleepless Nights* published by Finishing Line Press. Maggie co-hosts Poetry Street, a monthly poetry venue in Riverhead, NY.

**Carlo Frank Calo** the grandson of Sicilian immigrants, a husband, father and grandfather. He was born in Harlem, raised in the Bronx projects and is retired on LI. When not fishing, playing poker, counseling TBI survivors part-time or babysitting his grandchildren, he enjoys writing eclectically. 1170boy@optonline.net

**Paula Camacho** moderates the Farmingdale Poetry Group. She is President of the NCPLS www.ncplsociety.com. She has published three books, *Hidden Between Branches, Choice, More Than Clouds;* and four chapbooks, *The Short Lives of Giants, November's Diary, In Short,* and *Letters.*

**Loren Camberato** is a mixed media artist who currently resides in Lake Grove, NY. Her work spans from sculpture, painting, photography, producing local theater, costume design assisting, to creative writing and more. Loren is currently in pursuit of her BA in Studio Art with a minor in Art History at Stony Brook University.

**Lynne Cannon** is from Northport, NY. She writes poetry and has also completed two novels she hopes to publish soon. She is extremely pleased to be part of the great poetry community on Long Island, and also to be included in this volume along with her daughter, Julia Menges.

**Christina Canzoneri** is a poet and visual artist, and has been published in various editions of the San Fernando Poetry Journal. She is a self-employed web designer, graphic artist, and a docent at The Heckscher Museum of Art. Christina resides in Huntington Station with her husband, Sal. http://www.poemetry.com

**Kenny Carr** lives in Holtsville with his girlfriend, Angela, and their dog, Baxter. He wrote "Tinkerman" in loving memory of his father, Charles J. Carr.

**Caterina de Chirico** makes her home on Long Island in the lovely seaside town of Northport where she draws inspiration daily. You can find more of her Poetry and Art on Facebook and Fineartamerica.com

**Anne Coen** is a special education teacher. Being a teacher, she thought someone was taking attendance at open mic and promptly signed the clipboard. Eventually this resulted in becoming a featured reader at Sip This, Bellmore Bean, Bellmore Library, and Oceanside Gazebo. She recently placed first in the 23rd Annual PPA Poetry Contest.

**Joseph Coen** is the other half of a poetic duo with his wife, Anne, and an aspiring painter. He is the father of a free spirit and senior airman. He has been published in *Bards Annual 2015, 2016, 2018*; and *PPA Literary Review #19* and *#20*.

**Jamie Ann Colangelo** is the mother of twins, Liane and Christopher, now adults. She is the author of *From The Father's Heart - A Book of Poems and Suggested Gifts To Inspire, Encourage and Bless Those in Your Circle of Influence*. She found her passion for poetry at the age of 12 and now enjoys encouraging others on life's journey.

**Anne Coltman**'s love of the arts and family has inspired her writing of two poetry books: *For the Love of Grandma and Charming Expressions: Capturing Life, Recalling Times & Enjoying Nature*; and two novels: *Scarred with Fortune* and *The Mute's Masquerade*. Anne is currently the Vice-President of the Long Island Authors Group.

**Lorraine Conlin** is the Nassau County Poet Laureate Emeritus (2015-2017), Vice President of the NCPLS, and Events Coordinator for PPA. Her poems have been published nationally, internationally in anthologies and literary reviews.

**Jane Connelly** is an artist, writer, graduate nurse and former legal assistant who lived in Guam, before moving to LI. Publications include *Avocet, Bards Annual, NCPLS Review, Oberon*, and *PPA*. Her book, *Beautiful Bellmore,* a pictorial 1950s history/memoir, is condensed on tape at the American Folklore Center, at the Library of Congress.

**Paula Curci** is a spoken word artist, poet, educator, and award-winning radio show host for "Calliope's Corner - The Place Where Poets and Songwriters Meet" on WRHU.ORG & 88.7fm. She has 2 spoken word CD's with the Acoustic Poets Network® and is the author of a chapbook, *One Woman's Cathartic Release in Poetry.*"

**Max Dawson** works full-time with adults with mental illness. Dawson is better defined by his interests in The *Civil War, The Transcontinental Railroad,* trains of that very era, day to day life in that very era, medieval history, and most importantly, writing. He has written for *Back-Row Cinemas*, a site reviewing movies and films—old and new.

**Kate Dellis-Stover** is a Columbia graduate with a B.A. in Literature/Writing. As part of a Bill Moyers' special called "The Language of Life," She read her original poem "The Slide Show" on Channel Thirteen. She has been published in a number of Bards Annual publications and has celebrated with the Bards and friends annually. She has facilitated many journaling workshops and has been a Key-Note speaker at mental health conferences.

**M. A. Dennis**, author of the book, *The Many Attitudes of Dennis: Spoken Word* Poems, has a journalism degree from St. John's University and been published by *The New York Times, Daily News, Madness Muse Press* and *The Pangolin Review*. He has performed poetry from Nassau Coliseum to Canada to Hofstra University.

**David Dickman** is a native of LI, and wrote his first poem in the early 1960s, which has (hopefully) been lost permanently. His interest was rekindled as a freshman in high school and it has been a nuisance ever since.

**Linda Trott Dickman, Bard's Laureate 2017-2019**, author of *Robes: The Art of Being Covered* and *The Air That I Breathe,* serves on the Bards Initiative board and is poetry coordinator for Northport Arts Coalition. She teaches poetry to children and co-leads an adult poetry workshop at Samantha's Li'l Bit O' Heaven coffee house.

**Anthony Dimatteo**'s current book of poems, *In Defense of Puppets,* has been hailed as, "a rare collection, establishing a stunningly new poetic" (*Cider Press Review*). He defends the mysteries of writing, art and literature at the New York Institute of Technology where he is a professor of English.

**Susan Grathwohl Dingle** graduated from the Program for Writers at the University of Illinois at Chicago, and has been published widely. She is also a licensed clinical social worker in private practice. Her website is www.susandingle.com.

**Sharon Dockweiler** runs a weekly creative writers' workshop at Brentwood Public Library. Her poems, essays, and fiction tackle tough subjects with wit and flair.

**Terryl Donovan** is an educator and writer who is spending retirement getting reacquainted with the Muse. She is grateful to her husband, Robert, who urged her to keep following the dream and her fellow writers at the Art Students League who inspire her.

**William Doyle** recently graduated from Northport High School and will be attending the University of Massachusetts at Lowell this fall. Having taken an interest in literature at a young age, William had naturally progressed from writing prose to sculpting poetry. He believes that poetry is the best medium to express thoughts and emotions.

**Peter V. Dugan**, Nassau County Poet Laureate, NY (2017-19), has published six collections of poetry and co-edited *Long Island Sounds 2015* and *Writing Outside the Lines* poetry anthologies. He has received HM from the American Academy of Poetry, LI Bards Poet Mentor Award, twice nominated for a Pushcart. He hosts at Oceanside Library.

**Ronald Edwards** has had many successes and failures. His personal life has been a roller coaster of highs and lows. Ron found that he had to be willing to do what was suggested and have a belief in a higher power.

**Alex Edwards-Bourdrez**'s poetry has won prizes in regional contests and been published in *Bards Annual* and *PPA Literary Review*. He is a former teacher of French Literature, and a public relations executive. He works with people with developmental disabilities, and directs and acts in LI community theaters.

**John Farrington** is a Medical Doctor and a professor of Anatomy and Physiology. He has been enamored by, and a proponent of, the arts and classics, beginning at a very young age. He will continue to support people's participation in endeavors such as this well into the future.

**Kerry Fastenau** is a native of Massapequa, NY. Inspiration for all creative endeavors is drawn from nature, new adventures and common human behavior. She loves to string beautiful words together. Kerry also gardens, is active in cat/kitten rescue on LI, and fosters monarch butterflies in the summer.

**Carlita Field-Hernandez** is a Spoken Word Poet based in NY. With a style all her own, Carlita will take her listeners on an emotional ride as she turns stories of her past into poems. She has been performing in NYC and LI since 2015.

**Melissa E. Filippelli** is a Long Islander, born and raised. She writes because she must and because she finds a unique comfort, strength, and voice with each penned word. You can find her poetry in *Poets to Come*, an anthology in honor of Walt Whitman and his legacy.

**Adam D. Fisher** is the author of poetry, stories, and liturgy. He has published four books of poetry: *Rooms, Airy Rooms, Dancing Alone, Enough to Stop the Heart,* and *Hanging Out With God.* He was Poetry

Editor (2006-2014) of the CCAR Journal, the Journal of the Central Conference of American Rabbis.

**Kate Fox** is a mother, breast cancer survivor, and award-winning author of the collections *My Pink Ribbons, Hope, Liars, Mistruths and Perception*, and *Angels and Saints*. She is the host of The Kate Fox Show. www.katespityparty.com

**Grace Freedman** is 97 years old; this is her 2nd poetry publication. Her husband, Walter, is 99, served in the US Army and was in the 2nd wave at Normandy; he was wounded and received a Purple Heart. They have been happily married for 76 years, have 3 sons, 7 grandchildren, and a great-grandchild on the way.

**Glenn P. Garamella** was raised in Douglaston, NY, attended Queens College; BA in Philosophy, MA in Counseling Psychology; NYU Lifelong meditator, student of Eastern Religion and Spirituality. Married, lives in Huntington, NY. Son lives in Boston, MA.

**M. Frances Garcia** is a contemplative poet and photographer. She is also an adjunct professor of English at Suffolk Community College in Selden, NY.

**G. S. George** is the son of Cypriot immigrants who came to America in the 1920s. He was born in Brooklyn, NY, and as a child lived in Virginia, North Carolina and New Jersey. He was graduated from Rutgers University in 1963, taught English and eventually went into advertising. He currently lives on LI with his wife, Joan.

**Tina Lechner Gibbons** has been writing for more than 50 years and was recently published in *The Suffolk County Poetry Review*, and *Poets to Come*, Walt Whitman's Bicentennial Poetry Anthology. She is currently working on her collection of poems and hopes to be publishing a chapbook in the near future.

**Shilpi Goenka** is an avid artist, poet, writer and spiritualist. She was published in *Bards Annual 2014 - 2017, Suffolk County Poetry 2015, 2016, Poets Almanac 2016, NCPLS 2017,* a 2016 contest finalist for NaPoWriMo and NCPLS. http://fineartamerica.com/profiles/shilpi-goenka.html, http://silentsculptor.blogspot.com/

**Jessica Goody** is the author of *Defense Mechanisms: Poems on Life, Love, and Loss* and *Phoenix: Transformation Poems*. Jessica's writing has appeared in numerous publications, including *The Wallace Stevens Journal, Reader's Digest, Third Wednesday,* and *The Maine Review*. She is the winner of the 2016 *Magnets and Ladders* Poetry Prize.

**G. Gordon's** photography, poetry and short stories are inspired by her faith in God. Her work has been exhibited at the Creations Art Shows at OSA in NYC. She attended John Jay College in Manhattan.

**Aaron Griffin** is a 31-year-old Long Island native who is currently working as a warehouse club clerk, and self-training as an advertising copywriter. He was priced out of LI and fled to Charlotte, North Carolina. He writes fiction in his spare time. He likes Pokémon and trains.

**George Guida** is the author of four poetry collections: *Pugilistic, The Sleeping Gulf, New York and Other Lovers,* and *Low Italian*. Publications include *Aethlon, J Journal, Maine Review, Mudfish, Poetry Daily, Tishman Review,* and *Verse Daily*. He teaches at NYC College of Technology, and is an advisory editor to *2 Bridges Review*.

**Maureen Hadzick-Spisak** is a retired Language Arts Teacher, an award-winning poet, and author of two poetry books: *A Bite of the Big Apple* and *Yesterday I Was Young.* Publications include *Whispers and Shouts, Bards Annual,* and *Sounds of Solace.* She's a member of Farmingdale Creative Writing and Poetry Groups and The Bards Initiative.

**Geneva Hagar** was born in Brooklyn and lived on LI (Paumanok) most of her life, where she is inspired by the surroundings. She has a BA in Fine Arts from Stony Brook University and is the author of three books, *The Folk Art Poet, Moon Flowers* and her recent book, *The Silver Tree.* Geneva has been published in *Suffolk County Poetry Review 2019.*

**Nick Hale** is a co-founder and the current vice president of the Bards Initiative, and one of the editors of this volume. He has been writing poetry for most of his life, but his poetry career really took off in 2010 when he joined his long-time friend and business partner James P. Wagner with Local Gems Press. Since then, he has edited dozens of anthologies including *NoVA Bards*, and the best-selling *Sounds of Solace.* He is also the author of *Broken Reflections* and co-author of the best-selling *Japanese Poetry Forms, a Poet's Guide.* Nick currently lives in Northern Virginia where he hosts workshops, classes, and readings through his group, NoVA Bards. He also travels the East Coast teaching various poetry, writing, and publishing related topics. His hobbies include salsa dancing, salsa eating, and watching people laugh as they read his writing (or bio).

**Robert L. Harrison** is an award-winning poet, photographer, and playwright who has been active in the arts scene on Long island for the past twenty-five years.

**Gladys Henderson**, Suffolk County Poet Laureate 2017-2019, was named 2010 Walt Whitman Birthplace Poet of the Year. She is the co-editor of *Leaves of Me*, an anthology of mentee and mentor poetry in honor of Walt Whitman, and the author of the chapbook *Eclipse of Heaven*. Her poems have been featured on PBS's *Shoreline Sonata*.

**Judith Lee Herbert's** chapbook *Songbird* (Kelsay Books) was a finalist in the Blue Light 2017 Chapbook Competition. Her poems have appeared in *Bards Annual, Before the Dawn, NCPLS Review, LIQ, These Fragile Lilacs, First Literary Review East, Mothering in the Middle*, and *The Ekphrastic Review.*

**Sheila Hoffenberg** has been published in *The American Poetry Anthology*, *PPA Literary Review 2016*, and *Nassau County Poet Laureate Society Review 2018.* She won an honorable mention in the Princess Ronkonkoma Adult Poetry Contest and has been a member of the Long Island Writers' Guild since 2012.

**Arnold Hollander** publishes a quarterly magazine, *Grassroot Reflections.* He has poems in various anthologies. His poem, "A Penny For Your Thoughts," was nominated for a Pushcart award. His poems and short stories are in the online magazine, *Bewildering Stories* and he keeps a blog at www.arnieh.webs.com.

**Kevin Holmes** was Brooklyn born, married with six children; he taught 3 years elementary, 2 years high school, reading and writing. He's a believer, happy in life, dented a little. Kevin is a word inspector and collector.

**Terry Hume** has been writing since in her teens. Terry has been featured in *Bards Annual 2016, Bards Annual 2017, Nassau County Poet Laureate Society Review Volume V, Suffolk County Poetry Review 2017,* and *The Poets Almanac: A Poetry Lovers Journal 2017 Edition.*

**R. J. Huneke** has had poems published in numerous literary magazines and books, including *Unleashing Satellites, Suffolk County Poetry Review,* and *Bards Annual.* As a finalist in the 2018 Local Gems Press NaPoWriMo Chapbook Contest, *American Political Asylum,* his first book of poetry, received publication in 2019.

**Maria Iliou** is an autistic artist, poet, actress, director, producer, advocate, and host. Maria's been published in *Perspectives, Bards Annual 2011-2016,* and *Rhyme and PUNishment.* Maria is host for *Athena Autistic Artist,* which airs on public access tv and hosts the radio show, *Mind Stream The Movement of Poetry and Music.*

Dr. **Nurit Israeli**, a psychologist who writes poems, holds a doctorate in psychology from Columbia University, where she was associate professor of psychology. Nurit is an award-winning poet published in *The New York Times, Writer's Digest,* and other online and print magazines.

**Evie Ivy** is host to one of the longest running poetry venues in NYC. The Green Pavilion Poetry Event in Brooklyn. Her favorite book out is *No, No Nonets . . . the Book of Nonets*. Her upcoming book is *The Platinum Moon* from Darklight Publishing.

**Larry Jaffe** is the author of four books of poetry: *Unprotected Poetry, Anguish of the Blacksmith's Forge, In Plain View, 30 Aught 4*, and the soon to be published *Man without Borders*. He was co-founder of Poets for Peace (now Poets without Borders) and is a judge for the epic Arizona Poetry Contest.

**Kevin Johnson**, Johns Hopkins BA '72 (Humanities), Hofstra MS '05 (English Ed.); Member of Tudor and Stuart Club, Johns Hopkins Donor of rare book, Peabody Johns Hopkins Library. Gym rat, runner for 40 years.

**Gabriel Jones** is a writer, a blogger, and an influencer. He continues to discover who he is by reinventing himself daily. Gabriel believes that self-discovery leads to self-fulfillment which ultimately leads to a life full of experiences. Gabrielkjones.com

**Ryan Jones** began writing at an early age. Ryan's topics of interest include nature, human and natural history, mythology, and personal and collective experience. Ryan holds a bachelor's degree in English with a master's degree in childhood education, and works with children by profession.

**Evelyn Kandel, Nassau County Poet Laureate 2019-2021**, is a retired art teacher, BS Columbia, MA in art education, LIU; she is widely published. Two of her four published chapbooks have won top awards in national contests. She teaches an adult poetry critique class in Great Neck, and gives readings and workshops as one of "The Three Poets."

**Barbara Kaufmann,** a LI native, is a retired nurse whose haiku, tanka, haibun, haiga, and longer poems have been widely published in online and print journals. Her haiga, several of which have won awards, have been shown on the Japanese television show, NHK Haiku Masters. www.wabisabipoet.wordpress.com

**Daniel Kerr**, CPA, PhD, teaches accounting at St. Joseph's College and Suffolk County Community College and is also a lay minister in the Episcopal Church. His work has been recognized by the UN (Doing Business in a Multicultural World) and the Steinhardt School of Education at NYU (2009 Business Education Alumni of Year).

**Denise Kolanovic** is a poet and English/ENL teacher. She is active in many New York poetry associations and is the author of *Asphalt Sounds*, Foreangels Press.

**Carissa Kopf** is an inspiring poet who had published a number of poems along with a romance novella called *Time For Me*. When not teaching, her fingers dance across the keyboard creating more poems for her first poetry book. Carissa enjoys writing at coffee shops, beaches, parks, and/or right on her patio where she loves to garden.

**Mindy Kronenberg** is the author of *Dismantling the Playground,* a poetry chapbook, *Images of America: Miller Place*, a pictorial history/illustrated chapbook of poems, *Open*. She is co-editing an anthology, *Paumanok Rising Again: Long Islanders Reflect on Climate Change.* Poet, writer, critic, and professor at SUNY Empire State College.

**Joan Kuchner**, PhD, (Psychology, The Univ of Chicago), Retired Dir, Child & Family Studies, Dept of Psychology, Stony Brook Univ, has been honored for her teaching and writing on infancy, children's play and inter-generational issues. Today, she enjoys writing poetry, and playing with her 4 grandchildren.

**Kate Laible** is a writer, a photographer, and handy in many ways. She is a Managing Partner of The Firefly Artists of Northport, and co-founder of the Synchronicity Network Newsletter, which serves and celebrate Art, Science, and the Common Good on LI and beyond. She loves her family and making good things grow.

**Tara Lamberti** is a psychic and poet who lives in Head of the Harbor with her beloved Golden Retriever, Chewbacca.

**Billy Lamont** is a multi-media poetry performer appearing on tv, performed at rock festivals such as Lollapalooza, and on radio stations across the US. He has 3 books of poetry and 8 poetry with music CDs. His newest book of poetry is *Words Ripped From A Soul Still Bleeding.* He gives poetry workshops for students through BOCES.

**Ellen Lawrence,** great-grandmother, retired business owner, and animal welfare worker, has been writing poetry since she was 10 years old. She has written poetry columns for monthly newsletters and her poetry appears in many anthologies including *Bards Annual, PPA,* and others.

**Tonia Leon** is a bilingual poet who has published poetry and prose in English and Spanish in journals and newspapers here and abroad. She has two chapbooks: *My Beloved Chaos* (2013) and *Slow-Cooked Poetry/Poesía a fuego lento* (2017). She teaches Latin American Studies at CUNY.

**Sarah Losner** is an accountant who loves writing and performing poetry.

**Michael McCarthy** resides in Port Jefferson with his wife, Toni Ann. He teaches theology at the Mary Louis Academy in Jamaica, Queens. He is the author of a poetry book entitled, *The Ways of Grace*.

**Mollie McMullan** is an eleventh-grade student at Shoreham-Wading River High School. Her interests include painting, anthropology, and writing. Her life's experiences have formed a conduit through which her poetry is born. Mangled phrases appear, ultimately joining one another, in verse.

**John F. McMullen**, *"johnmac the bard"* is the Poet Laureate of the Town of Yorktown, NY, a member of the American Academy of Poets the author of over 2,500 columns and eight books (available on Amazon), and a radio host.

**Gene McParland** is a graduate from Queens College who has always had a passion for poetry. His works have appeared in numerous poetry publications over the years. He is the author of *Baby Boomer Ramblings*, a collection of essays and poetry, and *Adult Without, Child Within*, his collection on poetry celebrating the child within.

**Joe Maldonado** is a writer from Long Island, NY. He is the author of the poetry collection, *Subterranean Summer*.

**Lynda Malerba** has been writing for over 30 years. She likes to explore different topics in her writing and she is open to inspiration from limitless sources.

**Maria Manobianco**'s poetry books are *Between Ashes and Flame, The Pondering Self,* and her first Young Adult Fable, *The Golden Orb.* She was the Archivist for NCPLS 2007-2015. In 2015, Maria received a pushcart nomination for her Sonnet, "On Meditation." She received a BS from NYU and a MA from Adelphi University.

**Cristian Martinez** is a 6th-grader at Ronkonkoma Middle School, mentored by Robert Savino. He was published in *Bards Annual 2018,* and Mankh's 2019 Haiku Calendar. He won 1$^{st}$ place in Princess Ronkonkoma Awards for his poetry (2018, 2019) and prose (2018). His poem, "Glimpse of Tomorrow" won Grand Champion for WWBA.

**Julia Menges** is a twenty-one-year-old from Northport, NY. She is an alumnus of Johnson & Wales University, the co-editor of *The Maze*, a literary magazine based out of Providence, RI, and an aspiring writer of both poetry and Young Adult fiction.

**Susan Meyer** is a LI poet with a hope to further creativity as a healing modality for all ages. As a Holistic Counselor she brings a range of modalities to integrate choices for reestablishing personal power in a confusing world. She is a multi-cultural person who sometimes writes in Spanish, and appreciates many mythic traditions.

**Edmund Miller** Senior Professor of English at LIU, author of *The Go-Go Boy Sonnets: Men of the New York Club Scene* and two dozen other poetry books, most recently *The Screwdriver's Apprentice*, and of scholarly books and articles and of produced plays, some in verse. His published dramatic works include *Dueling Lady*.

**Lisa Mintz** is a multi-media artist in the fields of writing, photography, and pottery. She has led professional development workshops to promote focus and mindfulness through creativity. She lives in Dix Hills with her husband, and is a mother of three and grandmother of one.

**Brandy Moeller** is 14 years old and attends North Country Road School. She is a member of The National Honor Society in 8th grade and an avid bibliophile. She plays trumpet, field hockey, and Tae Kwon Do. Brandy has written a sonnet with the Wind as speaker of the poem.

**Rita Monte** wrote her first poem called "Italy" upon arriving in the United States at age 12. She has since won several poetry contests such as Princess Ronkonkoma. Publications include *Nassau County Poet Laureate Society Review, Bards Annual*, and *No Distance Between Us, Nessuna Distanza Tra Noi.*

**Jo Mooney** is a lifelong resident of NY. As a retiree she lives in East Meadow with her husband; they also have a home in Pawleys Island, SC. Being chosen to present her poem, "Good Morning World," has certainly been an honor and she is so excited to have been recognized.

**Peter Morrison**, a professor of English, started late in life as a writer of poetry. He has had several of his poems published in several *Bards Annuals.*

**Joseph Munisteri** is the digital curator of www.unlockcreativity.org. His first book of poetry is *Butterflies in Space*. He believes art in all forms should be accessible to all.

**Marsha M. Nelson** is a playwright, an award-winning poet, and the author of two poetry books, *Night Visions* and *All Rise-Stand Up Holy Gates*. She has written and directed several Resurrection Cantatas and Christmas plays. Publications include *NCPLS, PPA Literary Review, LI Quarterly, Poet's Almanac 2017, Bards Annual 2016, 2017.*

**Donna Nolan** is a mom of 3 amazing human beings, married for almost 21 years, and is co-author of a fictional, supernatural, "Blog Opera" entitled *Delilah's Coven*. She is Queen of the Red Hat Society chapter, *Sisterhood of the Crazy Hat Ladies, l*oves road trips, trying new things, volunteering, and spending time with friends and family.

**George H. Northrup** is the author of two poetry collections, *You Might Fall In* (Local Gems Press) and *Wave into Wave, Light into Light: Poems and Places* (IPBooks.net). He is a psychologist in New Hyde Park, NY.

**Joan Vullo Obergh** is a multi-award-winning poet, has been published in numerous anthologies and literary magazines, including *Lyric, Oberon* and as featured poet in *Avocet*. She has published a volume of poetry, *Rara Avis*, and an anthology of short fiction, *Chapter One*, in collaboration with her novelist writing group.

**Susan O'Byrne** is a native Long Islander who has been writing poems and lyrics her entire life. She is a high school French and Spanish teacher and a Recreation Leader for the elderly and infirmed. She has published four books of her poems. As a mother of 2 boys, she is especially proud of the storybook poems she wrote with them in mind.

**Tom Oleszczuk** has published in various journals and online, hosted readings in Brooklyn, Manhattan, and Sag Harbor. He now lives in Sag Harbor with his wife, Heidi, and their four cats.

**Rex Patrick** is a lifelong writer of fiction, short stories, poems and screenplays. He was born in France of Italian ancestry and currently resides in New York State.

**Marlene Patti** was born and raised in Chile; she currently resides in Selden, NY with her husband, Dan, and sons. She is active in her community as a volunteer for Town of Brookhaven Disability Task Force. She is a Licensed Real Estate Agent and loves to read, write, and hopes to become a certified Zumba instructor.

**Mary C. M. Phillips** is a caffeinated wife, mother, and writer. Her essays have appeared in numerous national bestselling anthologies. She blogs about books and poetry at CaffeineEpiphanies.com. Follow her on twitter @marycmphil

**Kelly Powell** is a graduate of SUNY Binghamton's Rhetoric program. She has performed widely on Long Island and NYC. Her book, *Posthumously Yours,* was recently published by Local Gems Press.

Dr. **Pearl Ketover Prilik** is a poet/writer/psychoanalyst; her writing includes several nonfiction books, editor of a post-doc psychoanalytic newsletter, and editor/participant of 2 international poetry journals. She lives on a barrier island on the south shore of LI, NY with DJ, her husband extraordinaire and Oliver, the humanoid cat. http://drpkp.com

**Nino Provenzano** was born in Sicily, and lives in the United States. He is Vice President of Arba Sicula. He has published three collections of bilingual poetry, Sicilian-English. His latest, *Footprints in the Snow*, was presented at St. John's University.
ninoprovenzano24@gmail.com

**Stuart Radowitz** teaches creative writing and critical reading at Molloy College. Publications include *Ascent Aspirations, Bard's Annual 2018, Blue Moon Literary and Art Review, Calliope, Cold Mountain Review, Dappled Things, Ginosko, NCPLSR, Otis Nebula, PPA Literary Review, The Avocet,* and *The Molloy Literary Journal.*

**Megan Ramírez,** is a self-taught poet, who was inspired to begin writing poetry in 2014 at the age of 33 by John Trudell, a Native American poet. She has had various poems published in *Native Hoop Magazine* and 2 poems forthcoming in anthology for an online radio program, Late Night Poets. She resides with her family in Bay Shore, NY.

**Karen Ranieri** is a published poet with a strong passion for poetry. She is excited for the opportunity to transcribe interviews for an author's upcoming book. Karen enjoys dabbling in photography; recently one of her concert photos caught the attention of singer/songwriter, Chuck Negron - Formerly of Three Dog Night.

**Christina M. Rau** is the author of the sci-fi fem poetry collection *Liberating The Astronauts*, which won the SFPA 2018 Elgin Award, and the chapbooks *WakeBreatheMove* and *For The Girls*. Her prose can be found on *Book Riot*. When she's not writing, she's either teaching yoga or watching the Game Show Network.

**Leslie Reed** began exploring poetry in her teens as a means of self-expression she could only find from within. She returned to it as a serious endeavor as a member of a Contemplative Writing Group for psychotherapists, engaging all her senses through the ancient practice of "Scripto Divina," a sacred writing.

**Barbara Reiher-Meyers** was the LI poetry matriarch; her weekly newsletter kept the poetry community celebrating the art of poetry. She was a board member of LIPC and TNSPS; she coordinated events for Northport Arts Coalition and Smithtown Arts Council and conducted poetry workshops. Barbara's poetry continues to inspire. RIP.

**Phil Reinstein** inspired by his late wife Marie, The Insurance Mon is now writing and performing his own poetry songs along with keyboard, accordion and {weak} voice. His politically {in}correct poems have been published in more than a dozen anthologies.

**Lauren Reiss** is a poet, author, artist, educator and energy worker. She is currently writing a book on healing and is certified in several forms of energy medicine. Her publications include *Bards Annual 2018*.

**Diana Richman**, PhD, licensed psychologist, has published numerous articles and chapters in professional journals and self-help books. Listening to souls' stories for 30 years, playing cello in community orchestras, and writing rhymes for special occasions has evoked her desire to express her voice through the musical language of poetry.

**Al Ripandelli** was raised in Kings Park, NY. He has published in several collections since his introduction in *Bards Annual 2016*. He is also the author of a poetry chapbook, *Hearts Window.*

**Rita B. Rose** is a multimedia artist. She is also the recipient of two Bards Literature Awards (2018) and is the 2018 and 2019 Poet Laureate of the LGBTQ community on LI. She is the author of *Veranda Sundown* (Local Gems Poetry Press, 2019).

**Marc Rosen** is the Treasurer of The Bards Initiative and lead editor of *Unbelief.* When not solving people's problems, he enjoys tabletop role-playing games and reading on his phone.

**Narges Rothermel** is a retired nurse, and an admirer of Rumi and Hafiz. Her poems are published in *PPA Literary Review*, *Bards Annual*, *Avoce*t, Mankh's Haiku Calendars, and haiku du jour. She is the author of W*ild Flowers, Rays & Shadows*, and *Side Roads*. She was the 2016 winner of Newsday's Garden Poetry Contest.

**A. A. Rubin**'s work has appeared recently in *Kyanite Press, Pif Magazine,* and *Constellate Literary Journal.* His story "The Substance in The Shadow" has been named a Fiction War finalist, and his story, "White Collar Blues" was nominated for the Carve Magazine/Mild Horse Press online short fiction award.

**Lady Samantha** is a writer of mystery, humor, science fiction, fantasy, history, and other genres; she is also a poet. She has published articles on Yahoo! Contributor's Network, in anthologies such as *Bards Annual 2018,* as well as in *Parody, Enigma, Asbestos,* and *cynicmag.com.*

**Robert Savino,** Suffolk County Poet Laureate 2015-2017, is a native LI poet, Board Member of WWBA. His books include *fireballs of an illuminated scarecrow, Inside a Turtle Shell,* and recently completed bilingual collection of Italian American Poets of LI, *No Distance Between Us.* Robert is mentor to the young poet Cristian Martinez.

**Andrea Schiralli** is an editor and education consultant. She helps students with their college application essays; giving them makeovers provides her with "a sense of control in a world full of chaos." She is addicted to Taylor Swift, the color pink, and anything that sparkles.

**Karen Schulte** is a poet living in Suffolk County. She has had her poetry published in a number of journals and anthologies. She is an active member of Performance Poets of LI. She recently published her first collection of poetry, *Where Desire Settles* which won the Writer's Digest Self-Published Book Award for Poetry for 2018.

**Ron Scott** currently serves as Executive VP for the Nassau County Poet Laureate Society, and serves on the board of The Long Island Authors' Group as Membership Chair. He is the author of two novels, *Face of the Enemy* and *Twelve Fifteen.* Ron's work has appeared in various poetry anthologies and was nominated for a Pushcart in 2016.

**Robert Seck** is originally from Ogallala, NE and was raised on a farm until the age of 12. Barely knowing how to read or write during his childhood, he took a long journey to live with family on LI; the passenger he sat next to on the bus introduced him to the poet W.S. Merwin; he credits that moment with falling in love with poetry.

**Harriet Slaughter** is a former actress, singer, dancer, and arts administrator. She now paints and is an award-winning poet. Her collection of poems and original paintings, *Ars Poetica* celebrates the imagination from a woman's point of view. Her art work has appeared in juried shows in NY and LI.

**Emily-Sue Sloane** Huntington Station, NY-based is enjoying writing, reading, yoga and exploring Long Island's natural beauty following her retirement from a career in publishing. Her poems have appeared in *Front Porch Review, Medicinal Purposes, Literary Review of the Performance Poets Association*, and *Creations* magazine.

**Barbara Southard, Suffolk County Poet Laureate 2019-2021**, is a visual artist and writer living in Miller Place, NY. Her work appears in numerous anthologies and journals, including a short story in *The Passage Between* based in Dublin. She serves on the board of LIPC and teaches poetry to students at Walt Whitman Birthplace.

**Dd. Spungin** Brooklyn native, Dd. Spungin hosts for PIN and PPA. Her poetry can be found in anthologies and in-print and on-line journals, including *Maintenant 13, isacoustic, First Literary Review East*, and *Fearless*. Spungin lives for love, prays for peace, writes for her sanity and will read anywhere for a cup of coffee or an Earl Grey tea.

**Toni-Cara Stellitano** is a holistic psychotherapist, artist, and poet. She is inspired by women, their relationships with themselves, and the beauty that is born of their healing. Her private practice is in Commack, NY.

**Ed Stever, Bards Laureate 2015-2017**, poet, playwright, actor, and director, Ed Stever has published 2 collections of poetry, *Transparency* and *Propulsion* and *The Man with Tall Skin*. He compiled and edited *Unleashing Satellites: The Undergrad Poetry Project*, and is one of the editors of the *Suffolk County Poetry Review*.

**Lennon Stravato** A native Long Islander, was a Foreign Policy Contributor for the Hill newspaper in Washington DC and is a screenwriter with three films currently in production. He is a lifelong writer, who has recently begun to find his poetic voice. His work deals with issues of love, faith, meaning, and meaninglessness.

**Douglas G. Swezey** received his BA in English and Art History from Stony Brook University, has written as a journalist for many weekly newspapers, was Managing Editor of *Government Food Services Magazine* and author of *Stony Brook University: Off The Record*. He serves on the Board of Directors for the LIPC.

**Wayne Thoden** is a gymnastics instructor, stand-up comic, writer, artist, photographer and web designer, featured on Authors Den, The Year's Best Poetry, and is the Author of the book *Fright Time Stories*. Wayne was also a $10,000 winner on Americas Funniest People. Wayne resides in Ronkonkoma, NY.

**J R Turek, WWBA 2019 LI Poet of the Year, Bards Laureate 2013-2015**, Bards Associate Editor, is 22 years as Moderator of the Farmingdale Creative Writing Group, twice Pushcart nominee, author of *B is for Betwixt and Between* (2018)*, A is for Almost Anything* (2016), *Imagistics* (2015), and *They Come And They Go* (2005). Poet, editor, workshop leader, PPA host, and poem-a-dayer for over 15 years, the Purple Poet collects dogs, shoes, and poems. msjevus@optonline.net

**Janet Wade** is a frequent attendee at various poetry venues. Her poetry is written to inspire and motivate individuals from a spiritual point of view. Each expresses her devotion to God and shows how He has used the challenges in her life to shape and refine her way of thinking.

**James P. Wagner (Ishwa)** is an editor, publisher, award-winning fiction writer, essayist, performance poet, and alum twice over (BA & MALS) of Dowling College. He is the publisher for Local Gems Poetry Press and the Senior Founder and President of the Bards Initiative, a Long Island, NY based non-profit dedicated to using poetry for social improvement. He has been on the advisory boards for the Nassau County Poet Laureate Society and the Walt Whitman Birthplace Association. James also helped with the Dowling College Writing Conference. His poetry is also used to autism advocacy, having appeared at the Naturally Autistic Conference in Vancouver and in Naturally Autistic Magazine, as well as his essays. James believes poetry is alive and well and thoroughly enjoys being a part of poetic culture. His most recent collection of poetry is *Ten Year Reunion.* He is the Long Island, NY National Beat Poet Laureate from 2017-2019. James has edited over 50 poetry anthologies.

**Jillian Wagner** earned her BA in Creative Writing from Dowling College. She is an active member of Fanfiction.net and is working on her collection of short stories entitled *13 Dark Tales.* She was one of the founding editors of *Conspiracy,* a genre fiction magazine at Dowling College. She is a certified paralegal and sits on the board for the Bards Initiative.

**Margarette Wahl,** a Special Ed Teacher Aide and Poet, is published in anthologies, and has 2 poetry chapbooks. She is a member of Bards Initiative, hosts for PPA, and on NCPLS as an advisor. She is an Ailurophile, Astrophile, Bibliophile, Logophile, Selenophile, Judeophile, Anglophile, Xenophile, and more philes that haven't been named yet.

**Herb Wahlsteen** has been published in *LI Quarterly, Great South Bay Magazine, The Lyric, Paumanok Interwoven, Suffolk County Poetry Review, Bards Annual, Form Quarterly, Bards Against Hunger, 13 Days of Halloween, String Poet* (2 poems translated from the French, 2 poems translated from the Spanish), and *Measure* magazine.

**Virginia Walker** is the poetry book author (along with Michael Walsh) of *Neuron Mirror*, sales of which support pancreatic cancer research. She's taught English at colleges in New England and on LI. Publications include *Light of City and Sea, Nassau Review, Suffolk County Poetry Review, Touched by Eros, Bards Annual,* and the *Humanist.*

**George Wallace** is writer in residence at the Walt Whitman Birthplace, writing professor at Pace University, and Suffolk County's first poet laureate; he is editor of Poetrybay, co-editor of Great Weather for Media, and author of 34 chapbooks of poetry, including *A SIMPLE BLUES WITH A FEW INTANGIBLES.*

**Charles Peter Watson** is a writer and multimedia artist, co-host and events coordinator for Poets Aloud at b.j. spoke gallery, and the author of *Netherworld Befalls* and *The Blue Moon Complexicon: One Giant Leap For Penmankind*. He's currently the host/producer of the "Gawdless Pawdcast" on Podomatic.

**Jill Watson** is an intuit artist, a poet, and creates in a variety of forms non-traditional graffiti, photography, mixed media collage, salvaged creations and pencil drawing, but she is also an artistic force behind written word and events; she is a self-described Jill of All Trades. Jill is based in Huntington, NY, but considers the world her home.

**Amelia Wells**, 14 years old, is a writer with interests in music and theater. She has won singing competitions, had central roles in various plays, and received an outstanding score for NYSSMA which prompted her selection for SCMEA. She hopes to use her writing talents for music.

**Marq Wells** was first published in 1981 in *Zephyr* magazine. Marq has also been published in *Bards Annual 2011-2018* as well as The North Sea Poetry Scene's *Long Island Sounds 2008 and 2009*. Marq serves as IT Tech, event host, and photographer for the Poetry Place since 2009.

**Jack Zaffos** is a retired Therapeutic Recreation Specialist. He is the author of *Songlines In The Wilderness*, and *Meditations Of The Heart*. Publications include *PPA Literary Review, Bards Annual,* and *NCPLSR*. Known as The Calendar Guy, he curates the PPA monthly calendar. His works have been characterized as Contemplative Poetry.

**Thomas Zampino** is an attorney in private practice in NYC. He and his wife have raised two daughters, four cats, two dogs, and various other domesticated creatures over the past three decades. He formerly blogged at Patheos and now writes reflections and poetry at The Catholic Conspiracy. Poetry is his second act.

**Donna Zephrine** was born in Harlem and raised in Bay Shore, NY, graduated from Columbia University School of Social Work in May 2017 and currently works for the NYS Office of Mental Health. She is a combat veteran who completed two tours in Iraq. In her spare time Donna plays sled hockey for the LI Rough Riders.

# Take a Look at These Other Exciting Poetry Publications!

# Japanese Poetry Forms
## A Poet's Guide

When people think of Japanese poetry, the Haiku is the first thing that comes to mind. But the Haiku did not become the Haiku we know until a thousand years after the first manuscripts of classical Japanese poetry were written.

Learn about the Renga, the Tanka, the Sedoka, the Choka, the Haikai, the Dodoitsu and others. Learn about the Japanese death poem tradition and read some poems by Zen Monks that are up to 700 years old. Learn the history behind the vibrant culture that gave rise to so many wonderful forms of poetry, and how to write them.

## A Local Gems Press Best-Seller!
## Available on Amazon.com!

# NoVA Bards 2018!
## An Anthology of Northern Virgnia Poetry

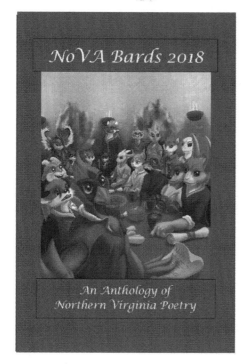

A collection of poetry from Northern Virginia poets.

Organized and edited by Bards Initiative VP Nick Hale.

NoVA Bards is the product of many workshops and readings conducted by the Bards Initiative's Northern Virginia Chapter.

NoVa Bards is the "Bards Annual" of Northern Virginia, take a look at what our brother/sister poets are doing!

Published by Local Gems Press
Available on Amazon!

# The Poets' Almanac 2019
## A Poetry Lover's Journal

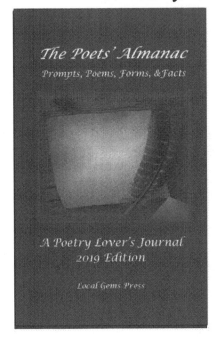

The Poets' Almanac was designed with the poet in mind. The Poets Almanac: A 30 Day Poetry Prompt Journal (With enough prompts to last at least 60 days) as well as ample writing space.

Information on poetry forms. Historical poetry facts Some wonderful short poetry Instructions on some NEW poetry forms An essay on how to plan a good poetry book launch.

Published by Local Gems Press
Available on Amazon.com!

# *Laurels*

## Poems by Long Island's Poets Laureate

Long Island has been blessed with various accomplished and invigorating poets laureate who help spread the art and encourage it. For the first time, their work has been put together in an anthology made easy for the average poet/ reader to appreciate.

Laurels features poetry by the various poets laureate of Suffolk and Nassau county, as well as a few thoughts from the laureates themselves.

## *Published by Local Gems*
## *Available on Amazon.com!*

A multi-purpose poetry project, The Bards Initiative is dedicated to connecting poetry communities, while promoting the writing and performance of poetry. The Initiative provides avenues for poets to share their work and encourages the use of poetry for social change.

In addition, the Initiative aims to make use of modern technologies to help spread poetry and encourage and inspire poetry, particularly in the younger generations. It is the core belief of the Bards Initiative that poetry is the voice of the people and can be used to help create a sense of sharing and community.

www.bardsinitiative.weebly.com

www.bardsinitiative.com

Local Gems Poetry Press is a small Long Island based poetry press dedicated to spreading poetry through performance and the written word. Local Gems believes that poetry is the voice of the people, and as the sister organization of the Bards Initiative, believes that poetry can be used to make a difference.

www.localgemspoetrypress.com

Made in the USA
Middletown, DE
03 August 2019